introducing mother and daughter, Gwen Hullah and Ida Barker - **your authors of this alternative book** - who established a book publishing partnership called, She And The Cat's Mother. At their core they are a " find your alternative " business

Whether you are looking for a foothold to start **climbing the property ladder**, or looking for a quick sale to downsize, or even a charity seeking new fundraising ideas to benefit the local community, together we are **sharing our research in this book**, hopeful it find friends, as we are the companions of our readers

This book acts like a kindness - it is inclusive, not exclusive. Its purpose is to be both generous and affirming - inspiring its readers to imagine possibilities and create an action plan to **think big and think differently** within current property markets

#OwnYourFuture

Share your story @RaffleProperty

Picture: (from left to right)
Gwen, Ida and Purrdey their cat

I0134946

@IdaBarkerDotCom

" Find your alternative "

Published by She And The Cat's Mother 2020
SheAndTheCatsMother.co.uk
Text copyright Gwen Hullah and Ida Barker 2020
Illustrations copyright Ida Barker 2020
All rights reserved

Connect to Team Gwen via:
www.silversplitter.com
www.facebook.com/gwenhullahauthor
www.twitter.com/gwenhullah
www.instagram.com/gwenhullah

Connect to Team Ida via:
www.idabarker.com
www.facebook.com/idabarkerdotcom
www.twitter.com/idabarkerdotcom
www.instagram.com/idabarkerdotcom

Photographs courtesy of the authors

Printed and bound by IngramSpark; powered by Lightning Source

Paperback ISBN: 978-1-9160474-4-0
Ebook ISBN: 978-1-9160474-3-3
Hardback (gold edition) ISBN: 978-1-9160474-6-4

Cover and interior design by She And The Cat's Mother

@RaffleProperty

RaffleProperty
Your Winning Guide
to House Competitions

for entrants, property-owners and charity organisers

written by mother and daughter
Gwen Hullah and Ida Barker

Illustrated by @IdaBarkerDotCom

Published by She And The Cat's Mother

Contents

find your alternative

Chapter 8 - Terms and Conditions document   113

Chapter 9 - Case studies   125

About the authors: mother and daughter partnership   141

Your notes   179

Chapter 1

own your future

" Inclusive, not exclusive "

Welcome

This! alternative book comes with a guarantee: it contains no mushroom treatment – meaning, you will not be kept in the dark and fed on bull manure

We, the authors of this publication, a mother and daughter partnership, have entered various Raffle Property and House Competitions, the purpose of This! book is not letting our research go to waste !! Our aim is to encourage and equip you to think big and think differently within current property markets

To combine, not divide, we write as we talk, using easy to understand rather than complicated language

Conversations are like stories, they're just the starting point

Raffle Property and House Competitions are not widely known about, but together, by championing them, and sharing our combined knowledge of struggles and successes, more events will reach their target number of ticket sales to cover the value of their properties. Therefore, more sellers will be able to transfer their property deeds and keys over to prize winners, rather than awarding smaller, alternative, cash prizes

Embark on a new course of action

Whether you are a budding entrant who fancies a flutter in a Raffle Property and/or House Competition; or, you are a property-owner who is seeking an alternative way to sell your property; or, even if you are the director of a non-profit charity who is looking for ideas to boost fundraising – This! property book has you warmly in mind

Each Raffle Property or House Competition has the potential to give generously by changing many lives – one at a time – but you have to be in it to win it

Together we aim to:

DISCOVER

REVIEW

SHARE

Wake-up, shape-up, step-up

In one bold leap This! alternative book will move the idea of social mobility from mere career choice, to gleaming actualities. Outlining guidelines of how to increase your chance of success on all rungs of the property ladder – whether you aspire to step onto the ladder, hold-firm the ladder, or climb upwards

Not letting the house get on top of you

The information within these following pages should be pressed into the hands of everyone – Raffle Property and House competitions are not well documented, but they are well imagined – from the year 2020 we enter a new decade. A new 10 years. The opportunity to learn from previous winners and organisers will help give us 20-20 sight in partaking and developing new property ideas and events

Valentine's Day House Competition WINNER

On February 14th 2020 "Win A Country Home" competition successfully awarded a £525,000 Shrewsbury property to winner, Jemma Nicklin

Incredibly, this House Competition was launched on 29 December 2019 and closed less than 2 months later, on the 10th of February 2020 (allowing 3 further days for free entries to arrive by posted mail)

Encouraging signs were reported from the beginning – while free tickets had as much chance of winning alongside bought ones, costing £2 each, it was stated on their competition website that – within just the first 4 days of launching the competition, they had already reached the half-way mark of ticket sales needed !!

"Win A Country Home" competition almost completed without interruption, at the last hurdle, they had to extend their closing date

13

from late January 2020 to the 10th of February 2020 – due to an unforeseen issue with their online payment system

However, good news was carried alongside this notification of change to the closing date, as they announced on their website,

QUOTE:

> "... we have passed this milestone [reaching the minimum requirement of 280,000 tickets sold] and will 100% be awarding the house at the live draw on Valentine's Day ..."

UNQUOTE

IMPORTANT !!
Raffle Property and House Competitions in a nutshell

In general, most countries, including the United Kingdom, United States of America and Australia view Raffle Property and House Competitions in separate ways: **a raffle can only be held by a non-profit charity** – therefore as a property-owner, you must look to partner yourself to a registered charity if you wish to go down the raffle route – whereas, **a competition can be held for profit by the property-owner** without any charity involvement

Reduce risk by taking personal responsibility for your actions

FOR property entrants >> always read the small print, often referred to as the Terms and Conditions document of a property event. If you are left with any bothersome doubts as to a raffle/competition's professionalism – avoid the event as clean as cold – and move on to researching the next up-and-coming event

FOR property organisers >> before applying any ideas within This! alternative book to your event, please seek legal advice from your local government/state's website. Laws in your country may have changed recently – avoid cutting corners – always take the time needed to read and understand new legislation

Bombardie (not Bob Marley): 3 top grumbles from entrants

Grumble 1:
The competition question is too hard

QUOTE:

> "... [House Competitions] they should try to keep their question / answer much simpler to encourage more ticket sales ..." —*Sandy Chamberlain's comment posted via Facebook, Summer 2019, regarding Win My Dream Home in Kentish Town*

DO YOU KNOW? It is a legal requirement to make House Competition questions difficult to answer – to find the reason why, and how to work-out the correct answer in future competitions, read Chapter 4

Grumble 2:
The free entry route is not free

QUOTE:

"... If you have to send a first class [postage] stamp then that can't be considered a free entry ..." *–Gwyn Carwardine's comment posted via Facebook, Summer 2019, regarding Dancers Hill House in Barnet*

DO YOU KNOW? The definition of a free entry can include a reasonable cost to the entrant as stated by the United Kingdom Gambling Commission – for more on this subject, read Chapter 2

Grumble 3:
The closing date has been changed

QUOTE:

"The closing date has been set back to February and you still can't buy tickets online!" *–Solveigh Grave's comment posted via Facebook, Winter 2020, regarding Win A Country Home in Shrewsbury*

DO YOU KNOW? Guidance from the United Kingdom's Advertising Standards Agency (ASA) states that "closing dates must not be changed unless unavoidable circumstances outside of the control of the advertiser make it necessary" – for advertising guidelines, read Chapter 6

This! Our alternative book must be read twice

ON THE FIRST READ be sure to write down your thoughts and ideas in "Your Notes" section at the back of this paperback/hardback book edition (if you're reading from our ebook edition – be sure to highlight text passages and record your ideas) then, formulate a plan of action to best suit yourself from the information you've read within This! book and research you've undertaken via the likes of expert, Google

To gain a full overview of how raffles and competitions work, we recommend you read sections for entrants AND organisers. By the time you turn the final page, prepare to see raffles and competitions in a different light. Prepare to let your feral flag fly

ON THE SECOND READ take action. Double down and allow This!

book to champion and spur you onwards as you put your actions into play

Our motto:
Warpentake = make your own opportunites

No longer does the language of property solely belong to established estate agents, building merchants or buyers-to-let – be more tiger-like: act fast, fearless but with fun. Take the alternative seriously, but don't take yourself too seriously. It is about the individual having the vision to make the ordinary extraordinary

Opportunity to do things has changed over the past years, mainly due to internet access – whereby everyone can now be an authority in their chosen field – this change gives way to a bold new order; an order taken by those brave enough to gasp the nettle of self-belief

So, by reading This! alternative book that shows less-traditional ways to engage yourself within the business of property, it will enable you to show you are part of the universal power of attraction – but remember, it's all a game. A game to win

The 12 game

The 12 game is a mission statement we created to help keep you on track when entering or creating a raffle/competition – it consists of 12 guidelines, 12 upticks as we like to call them – not 12 rules

The trouble with rules is they rarely suit us all. Rules are like promises. They can be easily misunderstood

HERE is,

The 12 Game

01. Go back to basics then find your alternative

02. Read everything, twice !! double-down

03. Skip convention; don't be careless, care less of following everyday rules

04. Hope is NOT your strategy

05. Plan close to the chest

06. Hugs — don't waste your reach

07. Instead of being a mortgage prisoner, beat the bank

08. Be yourself. More like yourself. Take charge

09. Lean into the moment and change will occur

10. Better to ask for forgiveness than permission

11. Make connections and inspire others to imagine possibilities

12. Keep your nose clean and your head clear

Like a salty breeze, you've sampled the beginning text – why not set your cap on This! explored book which falls into its determined space, and play the game, to WIN

@RaffleProperty

Chapter 2

starting point

" With grand preparation,
race out of the starting gate at lightning speed "

What do Raffle Property and House Competitions have in common?

Here are 3 similarities:

01. a ticket is purchased (physical or electronical)
02. a winner is selected at random from the entrants who purchased a ticket
03. the prize is signed over to the winner

NoteWorthy

if not enough tickets are sold to equal the value of the property within a raffle/competition once the deadline has expired, it is commonplace for an alternative cash prize to be awarded to the winner out of the monies raised – details of this alternative must be within the Terms and Conditions of a raffle/competition and all advertisements and promotions. This way you will help ensure it does not breach the trust between entrants and organiser

How does a Raffle Property differ from a House Competition?

To enter a raffle, the entrant isn't required to answer a question. Whereas, a competition must contain a challenging question, and only those who answer the question correctly will be entered into the draw for a chance to win

It is enlightening to know that a House Competition is classified as a prize competition, and can be organised commercially for private benefit and profit

Often prize competitions also include a free entry route whereby, for example, entrants send their contact details, along with their answer to the competition question in a sealed envelope via posted mail

According to the United Kingdom Gambling Commission, the option of having a free entry route is not a must have for prize competitions, but what is does state is that the free entry route must have as much chance of winning as the paid entry

Who can run a Raffle Property?

In the United Kingdom, raffles and lotteries cannot be run for any commercial gain or profit, such as selling your property or vehicle

The Gambling Commission and HMRC only allow good causes such as charities, local authorities and not-for-profits to legally sell tickets for raffles and lotteries, each entrant must pay to enter and the winner is selected through chance

Similarly, in the United States, a Raffle Property is considered a game of chance – such activity is illegal for a home-owner to personally organise one. However, a Raffle Property is permitted in the United States if the home-owner partners to a non-profit organisation who will sponsor the home raffle

2 routes to selling your property in a raffle

The quick-silver route

If you can find a charity to buy your property outright, a quick sale will be done – congratulations !! The charity will then either invest in the property, put it up for auction or hold a raffle. In the case of holding a raffle, their aim will be to sell more tickets than the property's purchase price to gain financial favour for the charity

The golden-glitter route

The seller, partners with a charity. The charity sells Raffle Property tickets in order to reach the seller's asking price and pay for the property

Once the raffle is completed, the charity will then award the property to a lucky winner, and the charity will benefit financially from ticket sales exceeding the property's value

Benefits to working with a property estate agent if planning a raffle

Finding an estate agent who is willing to contact charities as possible buyers for your property is not that dissimilar to the agent selling your property to an individual:

01. the buyer must provide funds to purchase the property
02. the estate agent will receive a commission once the contract is complete

The only marked difference being: the funds from a charity buyer may come at the end of the raffle when ticket sales are complete

Does permission need to be gained to run a House Competition?

NO !!

In the United Kingdom you do not need permission or a licence from the Gambling Commission, or a licensing authority, to run a House Competition

Why does a House Competition organiser include a FREE route of entry?

Main advantage

For many organisers operating international prize competitions, the liberal approach of English law is very appealing – choosing to run an international competition while following the United Kingdom law, namely the Gambling Act of 2005, highlights that while the Act does not regulate genuine prize competitions, it does permit prize draws so long as they are free to enter

a free entry route will expand the number of countries who can be included to partake within a house competition

The disadvantage

A free route of entry will mean less entrants are likely to take the paid route – after all, if you have the option of a freebee, where's the buzz in handing-over your hard-earned money, when the odds to win the prize are the same whether you pay or not?

The alternative: how to turn this disadvantage into an advantage

The House Competition organiser could link to a well-liked, registered charity by guaranteeing a price percentage of all sold tickets to the charity. This way more entrants will buy a ticket to benefit the charity – remember, the main focus is to sell a certain amount of tickets – if the sales target is not reached, then the House Competition will not be successful enough to hand-over the deeds and keys of the property to a prize winner, but instead, award a cash prize from a percentage of total monies raised after the closing date has expired

NoteWorthy

FIRSTLY, entrants buy tickets for a chance to win; SECONDLY, entrants will risk not winning to help a charity they like

House Competitions and FREE draws – a wise tale in detail

In the United Kingdom, House Competitions (also referred to as, prize competitions) rely on the entrant exercising judgement, knowledge or skill, and according to the Gambling Commission a competition must do one of two things:

01. the element of judgement, knowledge or skill will stop a large amount of people from taking part in the prize competition, or

02. the element of judgement, knowledge or skill will stop a large amount of people who do take part in the prize competition from receiving a prize

So, separate the chaff from the corn

NoteWorthy

if a prize competition relies on chance it may be deemed a raffle and could be illegal

Free entry, but at what cost?

A prize competition that also runs a free entry route for entrants, whether this is online, by telephone, or by posted mail, can incur a reasonable cost to the entrant, for example: the cost of purchasing a 1st or 2nd class postage stamp to fix to a posted entry is acceptable, but requesting special or recorded posted delivery is not acceptable as a reasonable cost

NoteWorthy

telephone communications – if a competition organiser makes no charge for entry but the telecommunications company does, over and above the normal rate that involves payment, as defined in the Gambling Act 2005, it is NOT acceptable as a reasonable cost

Free entry routes must ensure they follow these 5 points:

01. entrants can genuinely choose to take part without paying

02. the free entry route is no more costly and no less convenient than the paid route and charged at its normal rate

03. the choice of both paid and free entry routes are well advertised, so that it is likely to come to the attention of anyone thinking of entering

04. the system of giving prizes does not favour the paid or free

entry route

05. the free entry route is displayed with as much importance as the paid route

Benefits to working with a property estate agent if running a competition

House Competitions are organised by property-sellers (unless they pay an individual or company to promote the event for them), therefore having an estate agent independently value the property at an honest price will help assure entrants that the owner has not self-valued the property at an exaggerated price

The estate agent will also supply a detailed document of the property's special features, room dimensions, heating and electric statistics – details of which the property-seller can include within their marketing campaign to sell tickets

NoteWorthy

some estate agents will agree to evaluate the property for free and offer assistance with long sight that – should the prize winner decide to place the property on the open market, they will more likely become the listing agent

FIRST property WON in a House Competition in the United Kingdom

Brian and Wendy Wilshaw's property worth £1,000,000 on the Oldborough Estate (a fishing retreat in Morchard Bishop, near Crediton, Devon) became the first House Competition to successfully reach completion in the year 2008

In total the Wilshaw's sold 46,000 tickets; each ticket costing £25 to enter

The draw was briefly stopped while the Gambling Commission investigated whether or not to allow the draw to go ahead – however,

5 tickets were successfully drawn at the offices of a firm of solicitors in Exeter, and cross-referenced with the 5-figure codes allocated to each entrant who had bought a ticket

QUOTE:

> "We didn't want anyone to have any qualms whatsoever that the draw was not absolutely 100% legitimate, so we went with a low-tech option of numbers in a bag" *—Wendy Wilshaw*

Nationwide media attention

Following this win, the profile of House Competitions increased – people began to see an additional way for first-time buyers, up-sizers, or dream-home buyers to purchase property – the chance to win for the price of fish and chips, for 3 people, wrapped in newspaper

Media attention extended two-fold

Home-owners who had been unable to sell – some, due to a slump in the housing market, others, because they wanted to raise awareness for a particular charity – could envisage for themselves an alternative, a unique opportunity, and still be able to sell their property at a fair market price

*Note*Worthy

a property can still be on the open market while being a prize in a House Competition – it just means that if the property is sold before the competition closes, the property-owner will instead offer a cash prize to the winner

It's possible: a successful House Competition that didn't extend the closing date

YES !!

In 2017, Dunstan Low's Melling Manor, near Kirkby Lonsdale, Lancashire, worth £800,000 successfully reached completion without having to extend the competition deadline

The property was won by office worker, Marie Segar, who purchased 20 tickets in her hope of winning. And win she did – plus – a 12-month title of Lady Melling, given to her as a prize from the previous property owner, St John's Hospice in North Lancashire. This title was gifted as a thank you for a £30,000 donation from the Low family via the competition's earnings

In total, the Melling Manor competition sold an impressive 450,000 tickets at £2 each – raising a whooping £900,000

Within the first 24-hours of launching the competition, Melling Manor had raised £1,500 from around the world, and was beginning to gain media attention – a cracking start that began in April 2017 and led the way to this competition reaching success and announcing a property winner only 4 months later, in August 2017

Impressively, no time extension to the closing date was required. Dunstan Low's background in internet advertising must surely have been an advantage when organising this successful competition

FootNotes

for this chapter

=> raffles can ONLY be run by good causes

=> competitions can be run by property-owners for profit

=> no licence or permission is required (in UK) to run a competition

=> free entry routes will expand the number of countries who can partake within a competition

=> if a competition relies on chance it may be deemed a raffle and could be illegal

Chapter 3

what you will need

" Uplift voices are sensational,
but often go unheard as they're not sensationalism "

(a) entrants: entering a Raffle Property and House Competition

Access

Find a list of Raffle Property and House Competitions currently running. We set up a website called **www.RaffleProperty.net** which informs you of past and present property events

Research

Check out which Raffle Property and House Competition deadlines have not yet expired, and of these still running, which interest you. ALWAYS ensure you read and understand the small print – and only enter if you are fully happy to do so

Patience

Take your time to solve each House Competition question before entering, the reason being: competition questions will not be easily solved, the answer will not be easily found on the internet, and will not be easily known by the general public

They are planned in such a way, as to not equal an illegal raffle – whereby winnings are handed out solely due to good luck

REMEMBER, success for House Competitions depend on the entrant showing judgement, knowledge or skill. The question is NOT suppose to be easy !!

Entry

Some House Competitions only require you pay AFTER you have given the correct answer. This will save you a lot of money if you repeatedly offer-up wrong answers. While other competitions take an entry fee each time you supply an answer to their competition question – whether your answer is right or wrong

NoteWorthy

in Chapter 4 of This! book we outline common mistakes entrants make when answering House Competition questions – aiding you to become more savvy in working out the correct answers

Warning – red alert

Some. Let's repeat that word, SOME (note not all) House Competitions have come under the magnify-glass for writing in their Terms and Conditions document that a payment of stamp duty, council tax, ground rent and solicitors' fees is classed as a Discretionary Prize Bonus: awarded solely at the discretion of the organiser, and only if, the minimum number of ticket sales have been bought

Meaning, if the organiser only sells the minimum amount of required tickets, it has the option to award the property as a prize, while leaving the winner liable for stamp duty, plus all other costs involved in taking over and living in the property

3 startling FACTS of a Discretionary Prize Bonus regarding stamp duty on properties worth £500,000 (figures from 2020 regarding England and Northern Ireland)

01. if the winner has never owned a property before, they would have to pay £10,000 in stamp duty to move into the prize home;

02. if the winner has owned a property in the past, but is currently without one, or has sold their property with the plan to move into the prize home, they would have to pay £15,000;

03. if the winner wanted to hold onto their current home, and use the prize property as a second home or as a buy-to-let, the tax bill would be an eye-watering £30,000

However, some organisers go further to mention in their Terms and Conditions, that should a winner not want to pay stamp duty, they could, instead, opt to take a cash prize

Remember, the only surprise should be the winner's name, so ensure you:

ALWAYS READ

THE

SMALL PRINT

(b) organisers: partnering with a registered charity for a Raffle Property or, when setting-up a House Competition

Commitment

First and foremost: be determined to award the property to a prize winner. You should not enter into this project half-hearted. It is all about life-change (both yours and the winner – and, if applicable, a named charity)

Every decision must be built with passion and purpose to push you ever closer to achieving your end goal: successfully completing the raffle/competition

Duration

Allow the raffle or competition a timeframe of no more than 9 months, keeping publicity running throughout this schedule – it's a bonus if the deadline is brought forward because all the tickets have been sold

some competitions put in writing within their Terms and Conditions document that an additional period will be added onto the original closing date if the minimum amount of sold tickets has not been reached. Time extensions WILL cause disappointment from entrants, who then, often flex their views against a property event on social media

Communication

Ensure the raffle/competition is transparent – this point is so important, it is worth saying again:

ENSURE

IT

IS

TRANSPARENT

Communicate with clarity. Tell it how it is in an engaging way. Don't open the door to ambiguity or misinterpretation, otherwise you will let doubt fly in through the window. Plan. And plan well as to what you say and how you say it

Sociability

FOR Raffle Property – the charity you partner with may already have an excellent advertising agency that will market your raffle, for example: creating a new website to promote the event, showcasing images and videos of the property and taking secure payments for tickets online

NoteWorthy

avoid agreeing to your Raffle Property being simply added onto the charity's website – instead, you will need a new website created, solely dedicated to the raffle under the umbrella of the named charity – fail to do this and viewers will easily become distracted by additional posts published on the charity's general site, and in turn, cause many online visitors to not buy a single raffle ticket

FOR House Competitions – set up social media sites such as Facebook and YouTube, you must go to where people can share and discuss House Competitions with their family and friends to help create a buzz around your competition

Create dialogue by uploading videos regularly. Keep viewers in the picture as to how your week has faired. Ask them to respond to videos in the comments box, and join the fun by sharing your social media posts with their contacts. Be inclusive, not exclusive. Encourage them to spread the word. Help them make it easy to share

your story, and share in your story

Good causes

Connect to a charity you are passionate about to help the raffle/competition gain free publicity. Ensure the charity you choose has proper resources and manpower, otherwise you will end up doing all the hard work yourself

when shortlisting the best charities to connect to for your raffle/competition, here are 8 key factors to keep at the forefront of your mind:

01. choose a registered charity you like and believe in

02. look for charities in your local area, or those with a local division, they will provide a direct benefit on your community, rather than national ones

03. ensure the charities you are looking at are FUND WORTHY – remember, entrants are firstly buying a ticket to win a property, secondly they will take a chance not winning to support a charity's cause that they like

04. select charities that have an emotional appeal

05. check local media websites for which charities are receiving plenty of good stories

06. look for charities over 2 years old – the younger the charity, the fewer resources they are likely to have

07. check which charities have low paid chief executives and who are media active

08. select charities with a strong track record for raising funds

Network

FOR Raffle Property – if the charity you are thinking of partnering with suggests they can sell all the tickets by contacting their list of donors and sponsors – be very alert. It is unlikely to be that simple

Instead, seek a charity that reaches out beyond their current database. Check how active they are on their social media platforms, and importantly, how people are responding to the charity's social media posts

You will need a charity who is ambitious and looking to grow, not one that hugs what is close and wastes its reach

FOR House Competitions – plan how much you will donate to your supporting charity, and if this will be a percentage of the ticket, or a percentage of the overall amount in monies collected – (15% is a good figure to give to charities)

Remember, the more you can do for yourself in the running of the competition to lower your costs the better – you are spending other people's monies

Therefore, create your own website on WordPress. Start putting together your own social media content in advance: film short videos on your mobile phone and upload them to the internet; type-up a one page press release and email it to traditional media outlets (local and national newspapers and news programmes)

Learn to get a handle of these skills before your House Competition starts. If you have to pay someone else to do these things for you it can cost hundreds if not thousands of pounds/dollars

Empower yourself by researching other Raffle Property and House Competitions, note what you would like to change or copy – recreate or reinvent

Google anything you don't understand. All the while, embrace the learning of new skills head-on

NoteWorthy

a problem is never the problem. The problem is always people's outlook towards the problem. And outlook makes the difference between self-sabotage and adventure

Finance

Accept credit/debit card payments and cheques (ensure your ticket price will cover credit card and banking costs – more on these calculations in Chapter 6 of This! book)

Organisers: be in on it

2 raindrops, plus 2 raindrops don't always add up to 4, sometimes they make a puddle, therefore, ALWAYS research your district's laws for Raffle Property and House Competitions

Associates

Decide who will deal with handling the entries and how the prize winner will be selected (further details of this subject mentioned in Chapter 6 of This! book)

Legalities

It is commonplace that within the Terms and Conditions of a raffle/competition, the winner will NOT pay Legal Fees regarding the handover of the named property from the present owner to them – this will instead come out of raised funds from ticket sales. Ensure you know what that figure will be so you can set it aside for this transfer, for example up to £2,500 (see Chapter 7 of This! book for a Terms and Conditions template to help create your own small print document)

NoteWorthy

if your property is going to be repossessed by the bank, do you have time to plan, campaign and ultimately, complete, a raffle/competition? If the answer is no, it may be worth placing your energies into selling direct to a buyer/charity instead

Stamp duty calculations

It is worth knowing that the rate of stamp duty depends on where in the United Kingdom a property is located

England and Northern Ireland have the same rate. Whereas, Scotland uses a different rate band, as does Wales

Legislation brought in during March 2019, stated for England and Wales, new property-owners have only 14 days from completion (when all contracts are signed and dated) to pay any stamp duty costs, otherwise a fine and interest could be added on top of the overall cost

Generally, solicitors will take care of sorting out stamp duty during the handover, but it is the legal responsibility of the new property-owner to ensure the transaction tax is paid

The following tables outline stamp duty rates for the United Kingdom, and are correct for 2020:

England and Northern Ireland

STANDARD rates of Stamp Duty:
Pay no Stamp Duty on first £125,000
Pay 2.0% on £125,000 to £250,000
Pay 5.0% on £250,000 to £925,000
Pay 10.0% on £925,000 to £1.5 million
Pay 12.0% above £1.5 million

Scotland

Price of property at £500,000
Stamp Duty to pay is £23,350
The effective tax rate is 4.67%

Rates of Stamp Duty:
Pay no Stamp Duty on first £145,000
Pay 2.0% on £145,000 to £250,000
Pay 5.0% on £250,000 to £325,000
Pay 10.0% on £325,000 to £750,000
Pay 12.0% above £750,000

Wales

Price of property at £500,000
Stamp Duty to pay is £17,450
The effective tax rate is 3.49%

Rates of Stamp Duty:
Pay no Stamp Duty on first £180,000
Pay 3.5% on £180,000 to £250,000
Pay 5.0% on £250,000 to £400,000
Pay 7.5% on £400,000 to £750,000
Pay 10.0% on £750,000 to £1.5 million
Pay 12.0% above £1.5 million

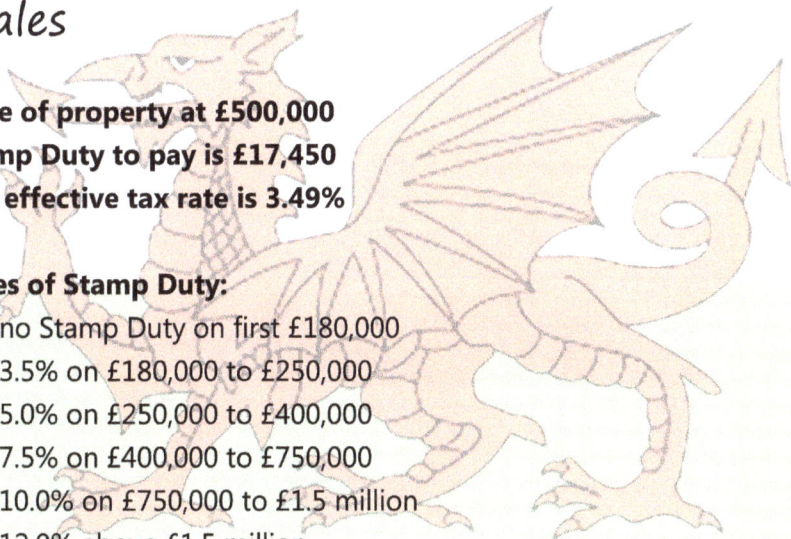

=> ALWAYS read the small print of a raffle/competition before agreeing to enter

=> ONLY registered charities that seek ways to grow – rather than hugging what's close and wasting their reach – should be approached by organisers

=> 15% of ticket sales is a good figure to give to a charity

=> Google anything you don't understand

Chapter 4

the formula used to answer
house competition
questions

" Risk and skill "

(a) entrants: which competitions to enter based on their entry system

You are likely to be asked one of three types of questions when entering a House Competition – none of which should be too easy. Remember, a House Competition is not a raffle, whereby your chances of being entered into the final draw depend solely on good luck. Instead – according to law – you will be required to show a degree of judgement, knowledge or skill

Types of question to answer include:

01. judgement – example, spot-the-ball in the picture
02. knowledge – example, multiple choice question
03. skill – example, mathematical question

To some extent, spot-the-ball competitions are a game of chance, and may be classed as an illegal lottery. However, if the competition is under English law, and if an organiser has included a FREE ROUTE OF ENTRY, the Gambling Act will permit prize draws (as long as they are free to enter) !!

The following pages show 2 examples of mathematical questions:

An example of an *easy* mathematical question

$$\text{🏠} + \text{🏠} + \text{🏠} = 3$$

$$\text{👍} + \text{👍} + \text{🏠} = 7$$

$$\text{🏆} + \text{🏆} + \text{👍} = 11$$

$$\text{🏠} \times \text{🏆} = \text{?}$$

The answer is 4

Explanation

LINE 1 each house is 1 as the total is 3
LINE 2 the house is 1, leaving 6 to be accounted for, so each thumb's-up is 3
LINE 3 the thumb's-up is 3, leaving 8 to be accounted for, so each trophy is 4
LINE 4 multiply 1 (house) by 4 (trophy), equals 4

An example of a **challenging** mathematical question

$$😊 + 😊 + 😊 = 3$$

$$✏️ + ✏️ + 😊 = 7$$

$$🗄️ + 🗄️ + ✏️ = 11$$

$$😊 + ✏️ \times 🗄️ = ?$$

The answer is 7 (not 8)

TOP TIP

multiplications must always be solved before additions and subtractions !!

Explanation

LINE 1 each smiley face is 1 as the total is 3
LINE 2 the smiley face is 1, leaving 6 to be accounted for, so each pencil is 3
LINE 3 the pencil is 3, leaving 8 to be accounted for, so a double filing cabinet is 4
LINE 4 multiply 3 (pencil) by 2 (single filing cabinet) this will equal 6, then add 6 to the 1 (smiley face), your answer is 7

(b) organisers: why MUST competition questions be so difficult?

As mentioned in Chapter 2 of This! book, House Competitions are also categorised as prize competitions. The United Kingdom Gambling Commission does not regulate prize competitions or free draws, therefore you will not be required to obtain a licence. But in prize competitions you are required to organise a competition that requires judgement, knowledge or skill from the entrant – this will mean the question you present to those entering must not be too easily solved otherwise your competition may be breaking the law if it is seen to rely on chance, and may therefore be classed as an illegal lottery

NoteWorthy

questions that are so difficult that entrants tend to guess the answer, can introduce a random element, and may well be classed as an illegal lottery !! The way to counteract this would be to include a FREE ROUTE OF

ENTRY, as under English law, legislation states that it will permit prize draws as long as they are free to enter

What are the downsides to creating a question that's hard to solve?

Many would-be entrants will be put off from entering your competition, and those that do, are likely to answer the question wrong. But, by law, the question must be sufficient to prevent a significant proportion of persons from entering in the first place, or, from eventually winning the prize

Record your evidence

While there is no guidance on what counts as a significant proportion, it is generally thought that 50% is enough. It is recommended, as best practice, to collect data by monitoring the activity of people showing interest in your competition, against the numbers that were then converted into entrants

An easy way to do this is to monitor your website's statistics/analytics. Keep a record of the number of people who visit your website from the time your competition is up and running to closing. Note, which website pages are viewed, and the number of entrants who complete your call-to-action by supplying an answer to your competition question. Not forgetting to note how many supplied the correct answer against those that got it wrong

Avoid questions with a game or prediction element unless you hold a licence

Never be tempted to introduce a question which has a game-element. Operating games for prizes is a regulated activity

Also, entrants who are asked to guess the outcome of a future event, such as a rugby match, is not advisable. This practice is regulated under betting laws

Do not shy away from challenge

There is no avoidance. The question you set in place must have a level of challenge, because if the Gambling Commission believe your question is too easy, they will not hesitate in taking action by shutting down an unlawful event which could also attract a fine and a prison sentence

How to safeguard against easier questions

If in doubt that the question you have set in place may be seen as a shade too easy, cover yourself by including a free route of entry

You may have noticed many multiple choice competition questions have an additional free route of entry besides the payment option for entrants – as stated in chapters earlier – due to English law, prize draws are permitted, so long as they are free to enter

FootNotes
for this chapter

=> there are 3 types of question to answer in a competition: judgement, knowledge and skill

=> when answering mathematical questions, remember: "multiplications have to be solved before additions and subtractions"

=> competitions that are too easy or too difficult can introduce an element of chance, and may be deemed as illegal lotteries

Chapter 5

open house events

Delorous Dival's three Ds to succeed:
" discipline, dedication, desire "

@IdaBarkerDotCom

Locally: on the doorstep
(in-person viewings)

One of the best ways to sell tickets for Raffle Property and House Competitions is through having an open house event – whereby the public can take a tour of your property and help spread the word to their family, friends and co-workers

Here are some top pointers to put into practice:

DATE – plan your open house events at the end of the week, Saturdays and Sundays, between 10am to 6pm when many people have the weekend from work

WEATHER – check your district's forecast and choose a dry day (with sunshine if possible)

APPEARANCE – ensure the property is clean and uncluttered, remove any valuables

STAGING – if the property is empty, place cook books, flowers and bowls of fruit in the kitchen. The aroma of newly-made bread should not be overlooked – people universally love the smell of freshly baked bread

For the living room, if you have an open fireplace or log burner: light a fire, also, find a homeware store that is willing to loan furniture for free, many will do so, under the condition they can display promotional catalogues and leaflets around the property

CHARITY – display charity posters around the property within large picture frames in noticeable areas – your mission is to clearly show images and information about your chosen charity's cause, and its achieved good work !!

ADVERTISE – hand out flyers and leaflets at your local shops and supermarkets and place posters around your town/city – do this no more than one week before the event otherwise people will forget

MEDIA – publish a one page press release, send it to news broadcasters both local and national. Avoid using abbreviations in the written word as it takes more effort to read quickly, also, abbreviations will alienate some people from fully understanding your message

SIGNS – create at least 30 road signs that will lead the way to the property

Write the fewest of words, and go-easy on using capital letters as they are harder to read

Put the signs up on the day of the open house event, covering at least one quarter of a mile in various directions from the property – ensure the road signs face on-coming traffic as drivers only have a few seconds to read them

NoteWorthy

write the signs in your neatest, clearest, boldest handwriting rather than paying to have them printed, the reason being – people are more likely to tune-out printed boards as they are commonplace, whereas the personal touch will draw their attention

HELPERS – people will begin to arrive at the property as soon as the first road signs start going up, ensure you have at least 2 well-informed volunteers at the property, who are able to answer any questions the public may ask, whilst the remaining road signs are being put in place

ENTRANCE – set up a greeting post here with balloons around the front door and a sign that reads:

In support of [<u>NAMED CHARITY</u>]

Set up an area close to the entrance with a table and a couple of seats, and ensure you have the following necessities here:

=> a banner displaying your website address for people to enter online;

=> paper entry forms;

=> pens;

=> flyers;

=> Terms and Conditions documents;

=> at least one portable credit/debit card payment machine;

=> a receipt book for cash and cheque payments;

=> wear a bag containing float money for entrants without the correct change;

=> a stapler with staples to fix receipts onto completed paper entry forms;

ARRIVAL – invite the public to look around on their own, at their own pace. No need to explain the Terms and Conditions in detail. Instead keep it simple

EXAMPLE GREETING

PUBLIC: Seriously, only £10 for a chance to win this house?

YOU: Yes. We're raising funds for [**NAME OF CHARITY**] by raffling this freehold house to be won by one lucky ticket-holder

PUBLIC: Ooh? So, for the price of a takeaway pizza we could be in with a chance

YOU: (laughs) Come in and have a good look round – we'd love to hear your feedback

avoid handing out flyers when people arrive as this can encourage them to return to their vehicles without taking a tour of the property, and, without buying any ticket(s). So don't give them an excuse to miss out

SAFETY – avoid letting anyone explore the attic or roof. The last thing you need is to call an ambulance to your open house event – although,

QUOTE:

> "[...] any publicity is better than none." *–Joan Collins, actress*

DEPARTURE – for anyone who leaves the property without buying a ticket: always offer them a flyer to take away. This will increase the chances of them buying a ticket online, or returning to your next open house event and buying one or more tickets then

always ask this open question* when people are looking to buy your tickets – "And how many tickets would you like to buy today?" This enterprising question will tempt some people to buy more tickets than they'd at first planned *open questions can't be answered with a dismissive one word reply, such as yes or no, instead they encourage the person to enter into a conversation

Globally: on the internet (virtual viewings)

It has never been easier to create high quality videos and short films with the use of mobile phone technology, and upload these creative results to the internet. Even within the established property business, sellers are encouraged to take video footage and photographs of their properties and pass them to their estate agents to market

With this in mind, there are 2 parts every property-owner should video and photograph: 1. the interior, and 2. the exterior

5 top tips to put into play once you have decided which areas to highlight

01. brightness – switch-on every electric light in the property

02. format – hold your phone in the landscape/horizontal position

03. height – keep your phone 5 feet high

04. space – video and photograph from the corners of a room for maximum effect

05. feature – start and end the video with the best looking room (avoid only showing the best room at the end of the video, as some viewers may stop watching before seeing it). Remember, the first and final images are likely to have the longest impression on the viewer. Don't waste an opportunity to sell the look. Take care of the little things and the big things should take care of themselves

there is great debate as to whether a video should be filmed by a mobile phone in the horizontal or vertical position – horizontal is preferred by many, but some believe vertical could be the future

The colour of a front door can increase a house's value by up to £4,000

On June 16th 2020, Channel 5's television programme, Jeremy Vine, co-host Storm Huntley mentioned a newspaper article that had caught her attention that morning, headlined, "Door Colour Can Boost Your House Price"

So which door colours came out on top?

According to the survey read out by Storm: black painted front doors could add an extra £1,000 onto the asking price of a house; whereas a blue door turned out to be the most favourable colour, excelling by an extra £4,000

However, a red painted door fell just shy of £2,000 when increasing a property's value. And finally, bottom of the list of coloured preferences, brown wooden front doors only boosted house prices by £700

<u>**View the following picture for "at-a-glance" reference:**</u>

Blue door   **+ £4,000**

Red door   **+ £1,800**

Black door   **+ £1,000**

Brown wood door   **+ £700**

*Foot*Notes

for this chapter

=> organisers should embrace BOTH offline and online open house tours

=> advertise an open house event no more than ONE week before, otherwise people will forget

=> keep road signs short and simple, such as:

Open House
WIN 4 bedroom home
tickets £4.99 each
101 Gladmere Drive

Chapter 6

raffle property & house competition regulators

" Listen to logic "

To summarise what we know so far ...

In the United Kingdom, the Gambling Commission regulate Raffle Property events. As mentioned earlier in This! book, raffles can only be held by good causes, such as:

> => charities,
> => hospices,
> => air-ambulance services
> => or other, not-for-profit causes

If an organiser has not properly set up the raffle, it may be deemed to be an illegal raffle and the Gambling Commission will have grounds to shut it down

In contrast, House Competitions can be run for personal gain and profit

Moving forward

It is suprising to learn, no single body is totally responsible for holding House Competitions to account. Because of this, they fall between the cracks of regulations

However, while the United Kingdom Gambling Commission do not approve or develop prize competitions or free draws, they can act where prize competitions and free draws are organised and promoted against the rules

In the United Kingdom there is a regulator called the Advertising Standards Agency (ASA). It is financed by advertisers and consists of people whose mission it is to protect the general public from false and misleading advertising

If the Advertising Standards Agency (ASA) identify a false-hood within a raffle or competition, while they do not have the power to prevent the organiser from running it, they will refer their findings to Trading Standards. But, it is worth noting, according to a report by the investigating consumer services body, Which?, Trading Standards are yet to get involved in such enterprises

Previous findings undertaken by the Advertising Standards Agency (ASA) include:

>> in 2017, a competition called homeraffler.com planned to award its winner the value of the tickets sold, minus 15% in administration fees. The Advertising Standards Agency (ASA) concluded the substitute cash prize was not a reasonable equivalent to the 'luxurious London home' and furthermore, by homeraffler.com failing to mention the possibility of a cash substitute in its original advertisement, it was ruled that the promotion breached the United Kingdom Code of Non-broadcast Advertising, Sales Promotion and Direct Marketing, also known as the CAP Code

>> in 2018, a competition by rafflehouse.com failed to include a

closing date within a Facebook advertisement, and also extending the closing date. The Advertising Standards Agency (ASA) concluded these actions breached the Code

IMPORTANT: the Advertising Standards Agency cannot stop an event running, but they can prevent it being run in the same way again – therefore, organisers have the opportunity to change how they advertise and promote future raffles/competitions in order to comply with the best practices

(a) entrants: avoid raffles/competitons that could be problematic

Do your research on events you are thinking of entering by seeking answers to questions such as these:

VERIFY – who is the event organiser? (remember, a raffle must be held by a not-for-profit cause; a competition must be held by the property-owner or agent/business working on behalf of the property-owner). Can you find any background information to validate them?

SUITABILITY – when looking at an advertised house competition – does it fall into one of two categories – a prize competition, a prize competition with a free route of entry?

TEST – ensure any house competition question you are researching shows a degree of judgement, knowledge or skill to be answered by entrants

ADVERTISEMENTS – has the raffle/competition stated in their advertisements what prize(s) will be won, and any alternative prize(s) if the raffle/competition fails to sell the minimum amount of tickets? (if not, they may be investigated by the Advertising Standards Agency which could suspend the raffle/competition's social media accounts if false advertising has been published on these channels)

DEADLINE – is the closing date placed on advertisements and within their Terms and Conditions document? (if not, they may be investigated by the Advertising Standards Agency which could delay the closing date)

EXTENSIONS – does the raffle/competition keep extending their closing date? (if so, it is unlikely the property will be won, but instead a smaller cash prize will be awarded to the winner)

NoteWorthy

the Advertising Standards Agency (ASA) says: "Stating the possibility of a change in closing date in terms and conditions of a promotion will not negate the need for a promotion to comply with the rule [...] and a change in closing date will still usually be problematic."

SMALL PRINT – is the Terms and Conditions document easy to find, and have you read and understood it fully?

HOLDINGS – is a third-party employed to hold all ticket monies collected during the raffle/competition? This is necessary to ensure the winner is paid out first, then the charity, and finally the organiser and property-owner(s)

CHARITY – what percentage of tickets sales will be going to the charity or will there be a cash donation? (15% of all monies collected is a good figure). Although, it is entirely up to each competition as to whether or not they are set-up in such a way to benefit a charity

SALES – does the raffle/competition detail the number of tickets they sold and other financial details, following the closing date? (if not, this may suggest something is amiss with the organiser)

IMPORTANT SO WE'LL SAY IT AGAIN always take time out and read the small print document of any Raffle Property or House Competition you are planning on entering. Do not waste your time and/or money entering one if you are doubtful about their professionalism

NoteWorthy

when it comes to job titles, organisers sometimes call themselves promoters

(b) organisers: primary rules to help you run a successful raffle/competition

These guidelines cannot be overstated:

01. all advertising and promotions must include what the winner(s) will receive; any alternative prizes; ticket prices (and free routes of entry if applicable); and the date of when the event will close

02. clearly set-out details within your Terms and Conditions document;

03. no details should be added or altered to the Terms and Conditions document once the event is running or has

expired;

04. you must run your raffle/competition fair and square

if a raffle/competition is deemed to be an illegal lottery by the United Kingdom Gambling Commission (UKGC), the organiser could face:

>> a fine of up to £5,000;

>> a 51 week prison sentence;

>> a 12% lottery duty for ticket sales and hefty penalties (via taxman)

Beware – Advertising Standards Authority (ASA) clause, 8. 15. 1:

QUOTE:

> "Organisers must award the prizes as described in their marketing communications or reasonable equivalents, normally within 30 days"

UNQUOTE

Therefore, according to the 8. 15. 1. clause highlighted above, organisers must award the financial equivalent of the value of the property as a prize

However, it is well worth mentioning, when Orchardton Castle failed to receive enough paid entries following their competition, a spokesperson from the Gambling Commission said,

QUOTE:

> "... it is acceptable with House Competitions, if enough entries are not sold, not to award the property, provided it is clearly listed on the site."

UNQUOTE

In other words, according to the Gambling Commission – if you do not sell enough tickets to equal the value of your property, you are not expected to award the winner a cash prize equivalent to the value of your property – on condition you have outlined this fact within your advertising, and your Terms and Conditions document – instead, a cash prize from tickets sold is a reasonable alternative to be presented to the prize winner

Furthermore, it is unrealistic to expect a property-owner who is running a competition like this, to have financial savings equal to the value of the property, and to then award these savings to the winner – when the reason most people take this alternative route of selling their property via a raffle or competition is to escape financial hardship. Factors such as: property prices falling due to a high level of people being unable to gain mortgages or, the market becoming saturated with too many properties for sale in a similar price bracket at any one time. Vital times lead to vital measures

Raffle Property and House Competitions give the seller choices, empowering them to make one of three market prices:

01. an honest price
02. a break-even price
03. a below market price

Not forgetting, in a downward economy charities suffer too – added pressure is placed upon their resources by more people needing use of their services, while local governments look to implement cut-backs and often react by reducing charity subsidies. And, on top of all this, the general public tend to give less towards charitable donations. Therefore, Raffle Property or House Competitions may help action non-profit organisations back into visibility by linking property events to charities in order to benefit their communities, with the potential to change many lives, one at a time

The best news yet

No property-owner has to wait for the cycle of down economies to return before heading along the route of a raffle or competition event

Even in an upwards economy, charities face ongoing challenges to raise monies – so there is no better time than now to start a Raffle Property or House Competition

No excuses
No pardons
No hesitations

Only alternatives

Plan it. Plan it well. And avoid calling this an experience. Experience is an excuse for failure. You must visualise success

NoteWorthy

the Advertising Standards Agency (ASA) has published guidance on their website specifically for win a house promotions

=> in the United Kingdom, raffles are regulated by the Gambling Commission

=> competitions fall between the cracks of regulators

=> if the Advertising Standards Agency (ASA) contact a property-seller regarding the 8. 15. 1. clause, the worst they can do is instruct the seller not to run their competition in the same way again

Chapter 7

the lucky prize draw

4 bedroom
house
ONLY £4.99
in support of ABC Charity

"Everyone's a winner"

@IdaBarkerDotCom

(a) entrants: buying tickets and entering for FREE (the price to pay)

The price of tickets will vary from one raffle/competition to another. The advantage of those more expensive is they require less tickets to be sold before they reach their minimum target number, whereas, the cheaper the ticket, the more tickets that will need to be sold. However, many entrants will buy batches of tickets if they are priced cheaper, say £2 per ticket, compared to buying only one ticket that is, say £75

So what is the best price to pay? When in doubt people often go for the middle ground – thinking it's the best bet – which brings to mind, advice clothing assistants like to utter, when customers find it hard to choose between the best dress to buy,

QUOTE:

> "Ensure it is tight enough to show you're a woman and loose enough to show you're a lady. This will take care of most situations"

UNQUOTE

The following pages show 3 examples of ticket price ranges, low, middle, high:

LOWER priced tickets
are between **£2** to **£9.99**

the cost of an
Eton Mess dessert

Photo by Ida Barker, featuring Nicola Isherwood
at Burgers and More restaurant, Harrogate 2019

MIDDLE priced tickets
are between £10 to £39.99

the cost of a
home-made cake

Megan's last shift in Home Shopping dept. Asda, Harrogate before working at a French ski resort

To wish Megan well we indulged in chocolate & cookies home-made cake by S&Ebakes Christmas 2019

Photos by Ida Barker
top left: Megan Cullen, Nicki Lofthouse;
top right: Megan's cake creation;
middle left: Lesley Bell and John Hunt;
middle right: Ant Hartas and Ida Barker;
bottom: messages of congratulations

HIGHER priced tickets
are from £40 upwards

**the cost of a group of friends
visiting a**

cat cafe

Photos by Ida Barker, featuring Kitty Cafe, Leeds 2019
(centre picture: Ida with friends, Corin Nelson and Simon Nichols)

(b) organisers: selling tickets, setting-up payment methods and creating FREE entries

How to issue tickets

Start researching businesses that will team-up with Raffle Property and House Competitions to issue tickets – 2 such businesses include, Eventbrite and Raffall – although there is no reason to issue physical tickets if you prefer not to do so

NoteWorthy

here's one advantage to not issuing physical tickets if you are running a House Competition ==> a ticket becomes void if the entrant answers the question wrong, and can therefore not go forward and be entered into the draw of correct answers – you may accumulate a lot of void tickets that cannot be played as the Gambling Commission states

The alternative to not issuing tickets

Hold a running catalogue (a list you keep adding to) that includes only correctly answered entries (this includes bought and free entries). When the time comes to select the prize winner, a good site to use is www.random.org

Once you have planned how to get the word out – into the public domain that your property is up for raffle/competition through your dedicated website; social media channels; press releases; and named charity – you must next work out how to take payments from entrants

Setting-up your payment methods

It has become popular for people to pay via their credit, rather than debit card. Many credit card gateways, such as PayPal and Eventbrite no longer support prize competitions (as mentioned in their revised Terms and Conditions) therefore you will have to seek an alternative, **your options include:**

==> go to a bank, discuss what you are doing and ask to set-up a bank account with them. To avoid high bank charges, request a personal account rather than a business account, remember, any such charges will come out of the monies collected from your ticket sales, so keep outgoing costs as low as possible. If you've exhausted all banks, and business accounts are the only option to you, then choose one with fewer charges, check out www.transferwise.com

==> if you manage to set-up a personal bank account, request for a current account with a savings account attached to it, this way ticket monies collected will be transferred into the savings account to help protect it. Remember, your bank details will be publicly online, transferring monies to an attached account is a secure way of keeping it safe. Discuss options with your chosen bank

by going down the route of personal bank account rather than business account, you may also generate for yourself a good amount of interest which could be donated to the charity you have linked to

==> it is possible to use mobile apps to take payments for tickets, though some companies will not exceed a transaction of a few pounds at any one time. Even so, it may be worth investigating this option further for yourself

NoteWorthy

have the aptitude? If feeling inspired, go to your local library and read books that will teach you how to create your own apps – not a library-user? – then Google it

==> make it clear if you are accepting paid entries via posted mail. A down side to this, if you receive a cheque without the entrant's contact details, or no answer supplied to the competition question, then these entries cannot be cashed

NoteWorthy

avoid accepting cheques from entrants in foreign currency as the charges to deposit them are high. If you are running an international competition, make clear – you will only accept cheques in your country's currency. It is advisable to direct your international entries to a provider, such as www.transferwise.com

Creating free entries

House Competitions must be classed as prize competitions or free draws. Free draws may gain you more publicity – **but remember, the entrant must supply an answer to the competition question, just as paid entrants do** – and only correct answers go forward to be entered into the prize draw. Fail to do this and your free draw may be considered a lottery and deemed illegal

NoteWorthy

the United Kingdom Gambling Commission state there must be as much chance of winning through a free entry as any other route

Options for entrants through free routes:

01. by posted mail on postcards (entrants must include their answer and contact details on the back of the postcard)

02. by posted mail on sealed envelopes (entrants must include their answer and contact details within a sealed envelope)

Globally speaking

It's the natural of the game, events such as these, run on the internet, will automatically make them international – unless you specify within your Terms and Conditions document that your Raffle Property or House Competition is restricted to a certain country

For example:

> "United Kingdom residents only, not international entries"

It could be recommendable to follow UK Law and exclude problematic countries, **otherwise you may need to consider the following:**

01. registering your raffle/competition
02. obtaining a licence
03. providing a bond or deposit
04. upholding a separate pool of national entrants from UK ones
05. making your Terms and Conditions available in other languages

Where to hold the winning draw and who to invite as witnesses

The options include: a local or national building or the prize property's yard/garden, if you have been carrying out open house events you will have an idea as to how many people may turn up to the draw event – think about car parking facilities, especially if it's the weekend

It is always advisable to invite people from the charity you are championing, local media, Mayor/Mayoress, legal advisors, estate agent and the general public, plus a well-liked local celebrity such as a weather broadcaster who will announce the prize winner

Create a raised platform from which the draw will take place and decorate the venue with a party-like feel – contact your local party shop 3 weeks before the draw date to ask if they will donate decorations in return for free advertising

Speeches

YOU: thank your sponsors [**NAME OF CHARITY**], your helpers and everyone who entered the raffle/competition, then explain the draw process with as much aplomb as possible

THE CHARITY SPOKESPERSON: must assure the audience that the Terms and Conditions document state charity members, celebrity guest, and any volunteers who are working with the property-owner, for this event, are NOT eligible to buy tickets for this draw. Information is to remain above board through-out the event. Don't let it fall by the wayside with careless words and actions just because the end is in sight. Maintain standards from beginning to end

THE LOCAL CELEBRITY: ought to sparkle when offering encouraging words to the audience before drawing the winning ticket. He/she should start by thanking the charity's good work in the local community, and remind the audience that whose who bought a ticket are already winners, as they have ACTIVELY made a difference in supporting a good cause. Then, he/she should identify how the charity will move forward as a result of the financial gift from this extraordinary event

What to do if the winner of the property is not at the prize draw event

The local celebrity should ring the winner and place them on speaker phone or video call them. This way the audience can witness and share in the congratulatory conversation – do not lose an opportunity to share with your audience the winner's reaction. You want to leave on a high if possible. It is all about having a memorable time for all the right reasons. FUN, being the operative word here

How many winners?

Some raffles/competitions have one prize winner. Others have the property prize winner and a few smaller cash prizes or holidays. Remember: however many winners you have, you must also have a runner-up for each one of them, in case a winner is disqualified by not being able to provide proof of eligibility

NoteWorthy

ONLY after ALL prizes have been drawn do you then

draw the runner-ups – avoid drawing them earlier, otherwise you will take away their opportunity to win a prize, and this may lead to complaints and a possible investigation of the way you ran your prize draw

Keep people happy – be fair, be square. From start. To finish

*Foot*Notes

for this chapter

=> the right price for a ticket is the price people are willing to pay

=> tickets can be physical and/or electronical

=> many raffles/competitions chose to follow English law as it is
   more lenient

=> a free route of entry allows more countries to partake in a
   competition

=> raffle/competition draws should be memorable for all the right
   reasons – fun, fabulous and informative

Chapter 8

terms and conditions document

" Avoid the mushroom treatment -
kept in the dark and fed on bullshite "

@IdaBarkerDotCom

Duel purpose

The small print: here is an example of a standard House Competition Terms and Conditions document – to be read with duel purpose:

01. if you are looking to compare against the documents of competitions you are thinking of entering, or

02. for those of you who are seeking inspiration when creating a Terms and Conditions document for raffles and competitions

in some Terms and Conditions documents an Organiser may be referred to as a Promoter. A Promoter can be the property-owner, an individual or company the property-owner has employed to run the event, or even a Charity sponsor

EXAMPLE of a
Terms and Conditions document

Terms and Conditions

INSERT NAME OF HOUSE COMPETITION HERE

The Organiser is offering Entrants via its Website the opportunity to win either the Property, or in the event that Minimum Sale Tickets are not reached, a Substitute Cash Prize

By submitting an Entry to the House Competition and ticking the box to accept the Terms and Conditions, you agree to be bound by the following Terms and Conditions

Each Entrant should retain a copy of these Terms and Conditions for their records

Segments

S1. Briefs
S2. Closure of Contest
S3. Contest
S4. General
S5. Privacy Policy
S6. Prize

S1. Briefs

CONTEST: The House Competition ran by the Organiser to which these Terms and Conditions apply, wherein Entrants submit entries via the website INSERT WEBSITE URL ADDRESS HERE or by post to win the Prize

CLOSING DATE: INSERT MONTH, DAY, YEAR HERE 12pm GMT. Free postal entries will be given 3 days grace period to arrive after the close of the draw

ENTRANT: Any person (not including a limited company, partnership or limited liability partnership) who enters the House Competition through the Website or by post to win the Prize

ENTRY: An answer submitted to the Question by the Entrant to obtain an opportunity to win the Prize

MAXIMUM NUMBER OF PAID ENTRIES: INSERT FIGURE HERE

MINIMUM NUMBER OF PAID ENTRIES: INSERT FIGURE HERE

OPENING DATE: INSERT MONTH, DAY, YEAR HERE

ORGANISERS: INSERT PROPERTY-OWNER'S NAME AND ADDRESS HERE

PRIZE: INSERT COMPETITION PRIZE PROPERTY ADDRESS HERE

QUESTION: The Question which Entrants must answer correctly to obtain an opportunity to win the Prize

VALUATION: (Estimated by INSERT NAME AND ADDRESS OF ESTATE AGENT HERE) INSERT ESTIMATION OF PRIZE PROPERTY FIGURE HERE

£???,000 plus stamp duty, and solicitors' conveyancing fees (inclusive of the Winner's solicitor's fees up to a maximum of INSERT FIGURE HERE + VAT)

WEBSITE: INSERT WEBSITE URL ADDRESS HERE

WINNER: The Entrant chosen at random on or after the Closing Date who will receive the Prize in accordance with these Terms and Conditions

S2. Closure of Contest

If the Maximum Number of Entries to the House Competition is unequal to the number of entries received by the Closing Date, the House Competition will close and the proceeds will either be deemed sufficient to award the property as a Prize at the discretion of the Organiser, or the remaining funds will be allocated as a Substitute Cash Prize to a Winner after the deduction of any expenses and marketing fees

The Organiser will be entitled to retain 5% of the Entry Fees to cover administration and marketing costs. The remaining balance following deduction of the 5% is "the Prize Fund". The Prize Fund will then be distributed to the winning Entrant

S3. Contest

Action to determine the Winner will begin the day after the Closing Date and a final decision will be made within 21 days of that date

The price of entering the competition is INSERT PRICE OF A TICKET HERE per entry and is payable using the "Buy Now" button on the "Enter Contest" page of the Website

By answering the Question, Entrants recognise that they must exercise judgement, knowledge or skill to give the correct Answer

To conclude an entry into the House Competition, Entrants will be asked to provide their contact details (including postal and e-mail addresses and a telephone number) and debit/credit card payment details. Once an Entry is submitted, the Entrant's card payment will be electronically checked for approval

Upon reaching the Maximum Number Of Entries or the Closing Date is reached, the House Competition will close; however the Organiser reserves the right to extend the Closing Date by up to 6 months at their discretion

All Entries to the House Competition are final and no refunds shall be made at any time or for any reason, except in the case of entries submitted after the Closing Date

The Winner of the Prize will be the Entrant whose details are randomly drawn at The Prize Draw Event before an audience of invited guests, members of the Press and in the presence of a solicitor. At this event, a Runner-Up will be randomly drawn following the Winner of the Prize, in case the Winner is later to be found not eligible to claim the Prize

The Organiser's decision is final and no correspondence will be entered into about the result of the House Competition following the determination of the Winner as described above

The Winner will be required to forward a copy of their passport or driving licence to the Organiser to prove their identity and that their Entry was made using a valid debit/credit card belonging to the Entrant or used with the express authorisation of the card holder

Each Entrant agrees that the usual requirement under the

Consumer Protection (Distance Selling) Regulations 2000 for any goods and services ordered online to be supplied within 30 days will not apply to this House Competition

If the Winner cannot be contacted by the Organiser within 21 days of being notified of their status as the Winner by e-mail, telephone and mail to the contact details submitted in their Entry, the Organiser shall be entitled to award the Prize to the Entrant selected as a Runner-Up at The Prize Draw Event ("The Alternate Winner"). The Alternate Winner shall have 7 days from notification of their status by the Organiser to communicate their acceptance of the Prize

The Winner will be required to sign a transfer deed to transfer the Property into the Winner's name within 28 days of Transfer of the Property

S4. General

Entrants may only submit their entries in the English language

By entering the House Competition via the Website, Entrants are deemed to have read and accepted these Terms and Conditions and agree to be bound by them

Upon entering the House Competition, all Entrants must submit all contact details requested by the Organiser, including a valid e-mail address, which will be used for the following purposes:

1. to inform the Winner that they have won the Prize;
2. to publish the Winner's name and town of residence on the Website;
3. to adhere with the Privacy Policy

All Entrants are solely and completely responsible for providing the Organiser with accurate and current contact details

In no way will the Organiser be liable for any failure or inability to make contact with any Entrant due to any errors, omissions or inaccuracies in contact details provided by Entrants or otherwise

The House Competition is operated by the Organiser

The House Competition is open for entry to all persons aged 18 or over excluding the Organiser, their family, agents, employees, professional advisers or anyone else connected with the development or operation of the Website or conductor administration of the House Competition in any way, shape or form

Entries made by Entrants to the House Competition will only be valid if made via the Website or as instructed by 1st class post on either a postcard or inside a sealed envelope

By entering into the House Competition, Entrants acknowledge that their payment of INSERT PRICE OF A TICKET HERE per entry to answer the Question and thereby enter the House Competition does not guarantee they will win the Prize

The Organiser does not in any way guarantee the value of the Prize

Only completed Entries will be entered into the House Competition

As a condition of entering the House Competition, Entrants must ensure that, by doing so, they do not contravene any laws of their country of residence. The Organiser will not be liable in any way if an Entrant enters the House Competition unlawfully

Entrants and the Organiser recognise that the House Competition, its administration and all associated activities are governed by English Law and Entrants and the Organiser recognise that the County or High Courts of England shall have exclusive jurisdiction in the event of any dispute arising out of the House Competition or its administration

By entering the House Competition, Entrants warrant that all information which they submit is accurate, true, current and complete. The Organiser reserves the right to disqualify any Entrant, if there are reasonable grounds to believe the Entrant has acted in breach of any of these Terms and Conditions

There is no limit to the number of entries that any one person can make via this Website. The Organiser is not responsible or liable in any way for the Valuation and makes no representation or warranty in respect of its accuracy

All Entries will become the property of the Organiser on receipt and will not be returned

All Entry Fees will be maintained in a separate bank account by the Organiser until the Winner of the Competition has been determined

The Winner agrees to allow the Organiser to display his or her name on the Website in accordance with the Privacy Policy. The name and town of residence of the Winner will be published on the Website for the purposes of announcing the Winner of the House Competition within 24 hours of the Winner being determined

Entrants authorise the Organiser to enter their personal details into their database and to use the information in accordance with the provisions of the Data Protection Act 1998 and subject to the terms of Privacy Policy

The Organiser reserves the right to cancel the House Competition at any time either before or after tickets have been sold. If the House Competition is cancelled, the Organiser will return the Entry Fees to each Entrant (either by bank card refund or by cheque and in one combined payment where several entries have been made by an Entrant). Where the Entry Fee is returned, the Organiser shall have no further liability to the Entrant or to any other person

The Organiser makes no representation or warranty as to the Valuation or the Prize, its structural or cosmetic condition or its ability to be sold. Entrants should make and rely on their own enquiries and legal advice about the Prize before entering the House Competition

Save for death or personal injury the Organiser will not be liable for any loss (including economic loss) suffered to or sustained by any person or property as a result of any act or omission of the Organiser, nor will their servants or their agents in developing, planning and administrating the House Competition, distributing the Prize to the Winner or following the distribution of the Prize

The Organiser accepts no liability for errors or omissions contained within the Prize details, description or specification or any other part of the Website. It is the responsibility of each Entrant (and in particular the Winner) to satisfy him/herself as to the accuracy of any such details and/or any content of this Website

The Organiser will not be liable for any loss suffered by an Entrant as a result of incomplete entries or failed computer communications or for any loss suffered as a result of use of the Website

The Organiser does not accept responsibility for entries which they do not receive due to failures in computer systems, other malfunctions, high internet traffic, hardware failure, software failure, server faults or any other reason

These House Competition rules shall not create or be construed as creating any form of contract, joint venture or other agreement between any Entrant and the Organiser

An entry shall be declared void (without any refund being given) if the Entrant engages in:

1. any form of fraud (actual or apparent);

2. fraudulent misrepresentation;
3. fraudulent concealment;
4. hacking or interference with the proper functioning of the Website;
5. amending, or unauthorised use of, any of the code that constitutes the Website

S5. Privacy policy

Entrants and the Organiser recognise that the Organiser may use contact details and other data including personal data as defined by the Data Protection Act 1998 supplied by Entrants to the Organiser to administer the Website and conduct the House Competition according to these Terms and Conditions

Entrants and the Organiser recognise that the Organiser may (either by choice or at the request of a third party) disclose this information to relevant third parties for the purposes of the prevention of fraud, money laundering, legal or other financial or regulatory reasons

S6. Prize

The purpose of the Contest is to win the Prize

The Prize will be transferred by the Organiser to the Winner of the Contest free from all mortgages, charges and other encumbrances, at the Organiser's expense and including all fees, charges and taxes

The Winner shall ensure that the Prize is registered at HM Land Registry in the Winner's name

Entry payments will only be accepted in British pounds sterling

Chapter 9

case studies

" Cheers "

Congratulations !!

You have reached the final chapter of this alternative book, wherein we highlight 3 House Competitions we entered in 2019 – ranging from lower priced tickets to the more expensive

Case study 1: Castle Competition

Photo: Ida Barker entering Hadlow Tower Castle Competition online

Competition prize:

Hadlow Tower worth £2,000.000 in Tonbridge, Kent, England, United Kingdom

Property description:

Grade 1 listed, refurbished Gothic folly with 4 bedrooms

Ticket price:

£4.50 (or purchase 3 entries for £10.50, or 10 entries for £27.50)

Opening date:

December 4th 2018

Closing date:

June 3rd 2019; later extended to December 3rd 2019

Sales aim:

to sell 800,000 tickets

Entry format:

mathematical question (pay even if you answer question wrong)

Entry question:

view following picture

Correct entry answer:

view picture at end of this case study

Free route of entry:

no

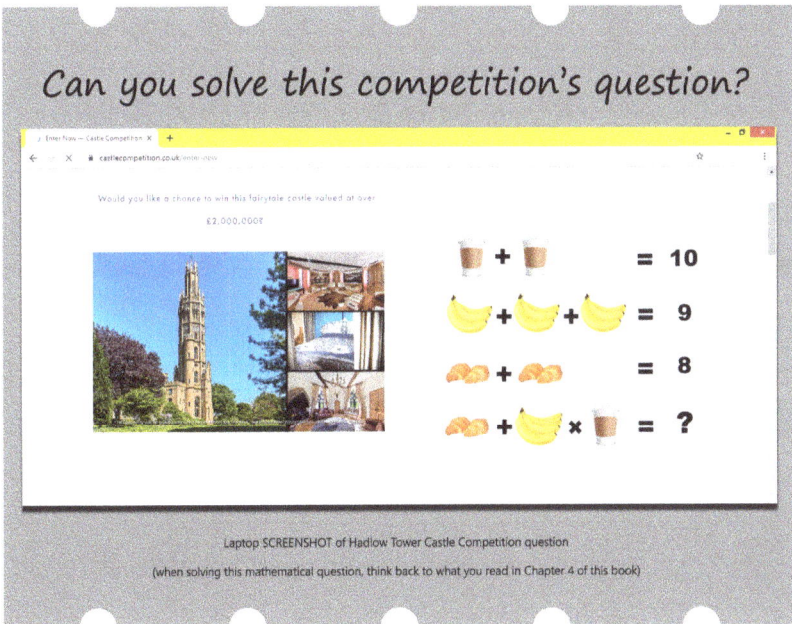

Can you solve this competition's question?

Laptop SCREENSHOT of Hadlow Tower Castle Competition question

(when solving this mathematical question, think back to what you read in Chapter 4 of this book)

Notes:

running alongside this property competition – whereby the winner can choose between Hadlow Tower or a cash prize of £1,000,000, or even a Caribbean Villa plus £250,000 (providing enough funds generated) – there were weekly prize draws for holiday breaks

Organiser/Promoter:

Myty Property Limited

Email communications:

as entrants we did not receive updates about this competition from the organiser/promoter

Competition results:

the winning ticket number was: 5c10d812a5ffc and as stated on their website, "The lucky winner has been contacted and has claimed their prize". However, it did not state what the prize was !!

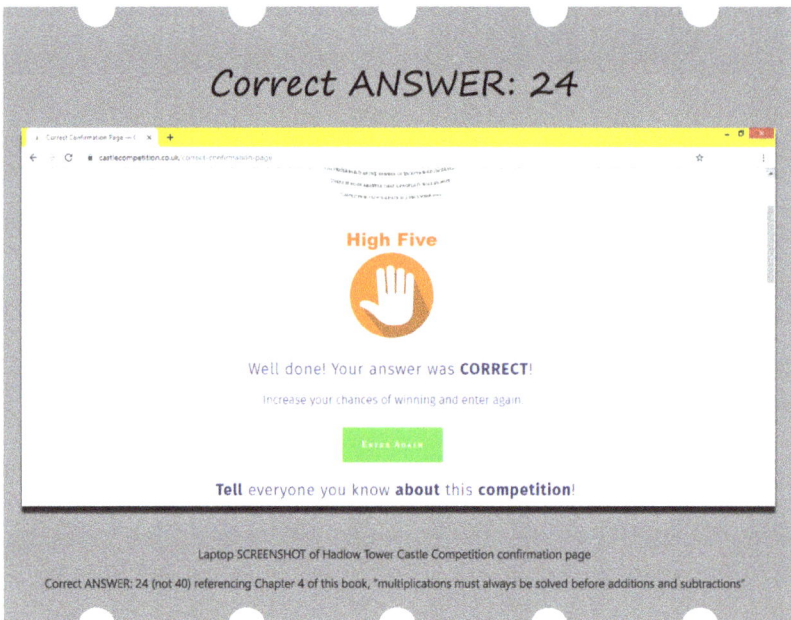

Laptop SCREENSHOT of Hadlow Tower Castle Competition confirmation page

Correct ANSWER: 24 (not 40) referencing Chapter 4 of this book, "multiplications must always be solved before additions and subtractions"

Case study 2: House Competition

Photo: Gwen Hullah entering Dancers Hill House Competition online (with Purrdey our cat)

Competition prize:

Dancers Hill House worth £5,250.000 in Barnet, Hertfordshire, England, United Kingdom

Property description:

Georgian Grade 2 listed property, boasting 6 bedrooms, cinema, gym, wine room and a lake – all set within 4 acres of land

Ticket price:

£13.50

Opening date:

June 16th 2018

Closing date:

December 2018; extended to June 2019; then extended to December 25th 2019

Sales aim:

to sell 600,000 tickets

Entry format:

multiple choice question (pay once you supply the correct answer)

Entry question:

"Who was the reigning Monarch, on Christmas Day, the year Dancers Hill House was built?" (competition's website stated the house was built in the year 1760)

Multiple choice answers:

(a) King George II; (b) King George III; (c) King Henry VIII; (d) Queen Anne

Correct entry answer:

view following picture

Free route of entry:

yes

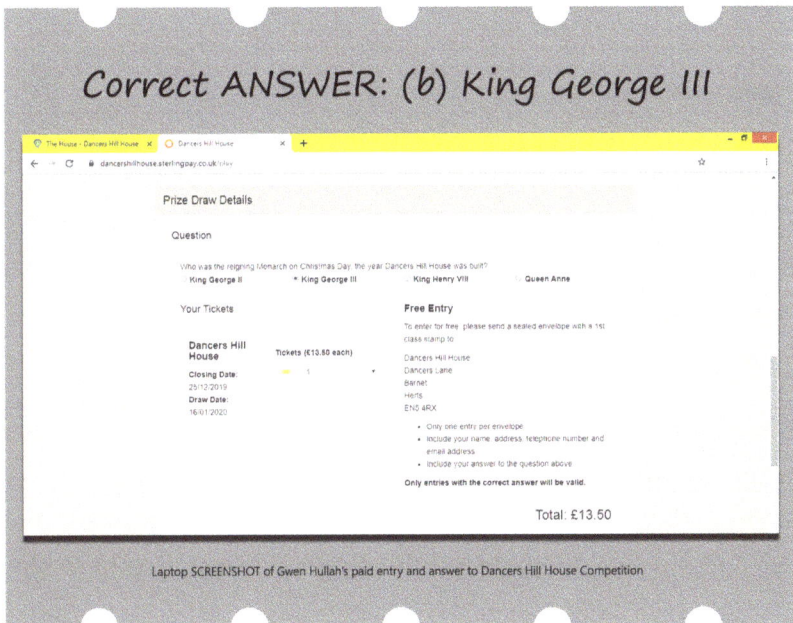

Correct ANSWER: (b) King George III

Laptop SCREENSHOT of Gwen Hullah's paid entry and answer to Dancers Hill House Competition

Notes:

Terms and Conditions did not outline the running costs of this property

Organiser/Promoter:

the property-owners along with Sterling Lotteries

Email communications:

good – as entrants we received updates about this competition from the organiser/promoter

Competition results:

the winner, a man from South London, who wished to remain anonymous, received a cash prize of 75% of all funds generated – insufficient ticket sales meant a property hand-over was impossible. The winning ticket number was: 21081810500126458-1

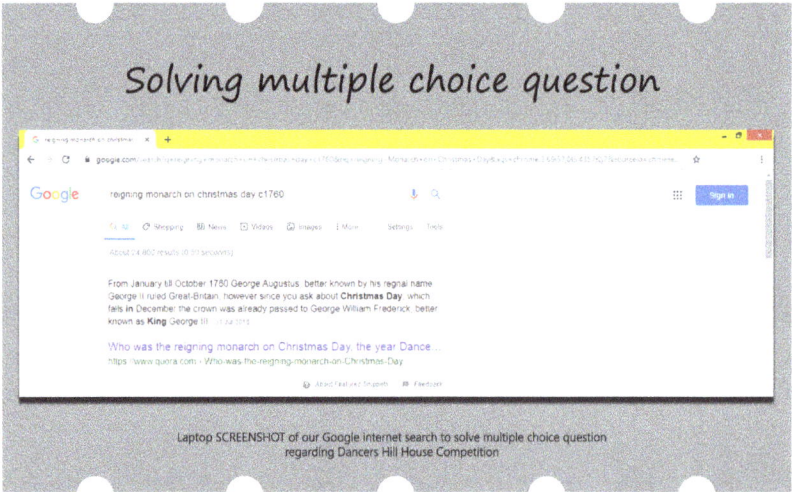

Laptop SCREENSHOT of our Google internet search to solve multiple choice question regarding Dancers Hill House Competition

Case study 3: Bungalow Competition

Photo: Ida Barker entering luxury Bungalow Competition online

Competition prize:

Bungalow worth £500,000 in Pangfield Park, Allesley, Coventry, England, United Kingdom

Property description:

recently extended and renovated luxury 4 bedroom bungalow

Ticket price:

£69.99 (or purchase 3 tickets to reduce the cost to £49.99 each)

Opening date:

July 8th 2019

Closing date:

October 5th 2019; later extended to January 5th 2020

Sales aim:

to sell 9999 tickets

Entry format:

multiple choice question

Entry question:

"What is the most expensive property on the UK Monopoly Board?"

Multiple choice answers:

(a) Oxford Street; (b) Park Lane; (c) Mayfair

Correct entry answer:

view following picture

Free route of entry:

yes

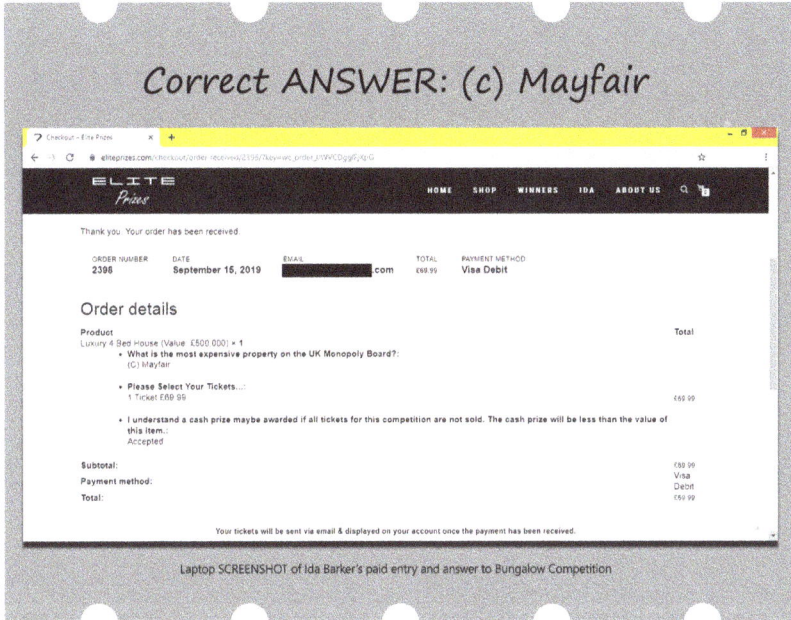

Correct ANSWER: (c) Mayfair

Laptop SCREENSHOT of Ida Barker's paid entry and answer to Bungalow Competition

Notes:

their Terms and Conditions document state, if insufficient tickets sales mean a property hand-over is impossible, then the winner will receive a cash prize of 60% of all funds generated

Organiser/Promoter:

Elite Prizes

Email communications:

as entrants we did not receive updates about this competition from the organiser/promoter

Competition results:

Elite Prizes posted to their Facebook page in January 2020 that they were suspending all competitions and were processing refunds. Their reason: due to new investment in their business they would re-brand as Raffle My Car

Competition entry refund

HSBC ◆ UK

Contact tel 03457 404 404
see reverse for call times
Text phone 03457 125 563
used by deaf or speech impaired customers
www.hsbc.co.uk

4 December 2019 to 3 January 2020

Your Statement

Account Name
Miss Ida Barker

Sortcode Account Number Sheet Number

Your Bank Account details

Date	Payment type and details	Paid out	Paid in	Balance
	BALANCE BROUGHT FORWARD			
20 Dec 19	VIS ELITE PRIZES			
	ELITE - HOUSE		69.99	

Photo: Ida Barker's HSBC bank statement showing full refund of £69.99 following suspension of Bungalow Competition

138

Now, with every ending there is always a new beginning

This is your plan B – create it; own it; share it

JOIN the conversation

Share your raffle/competition stories with us and others !!
We'd love to hear which property events you have entered or
organised, and what's been your take on it so far?

Join in on facebook | twitter | instagram

@RaffleProperty

And lastly ...

View the following pages to discover a little about the authors of This!
book, a mother and daughter partnership ==>

140

About the authors

mother and daughter
partnership

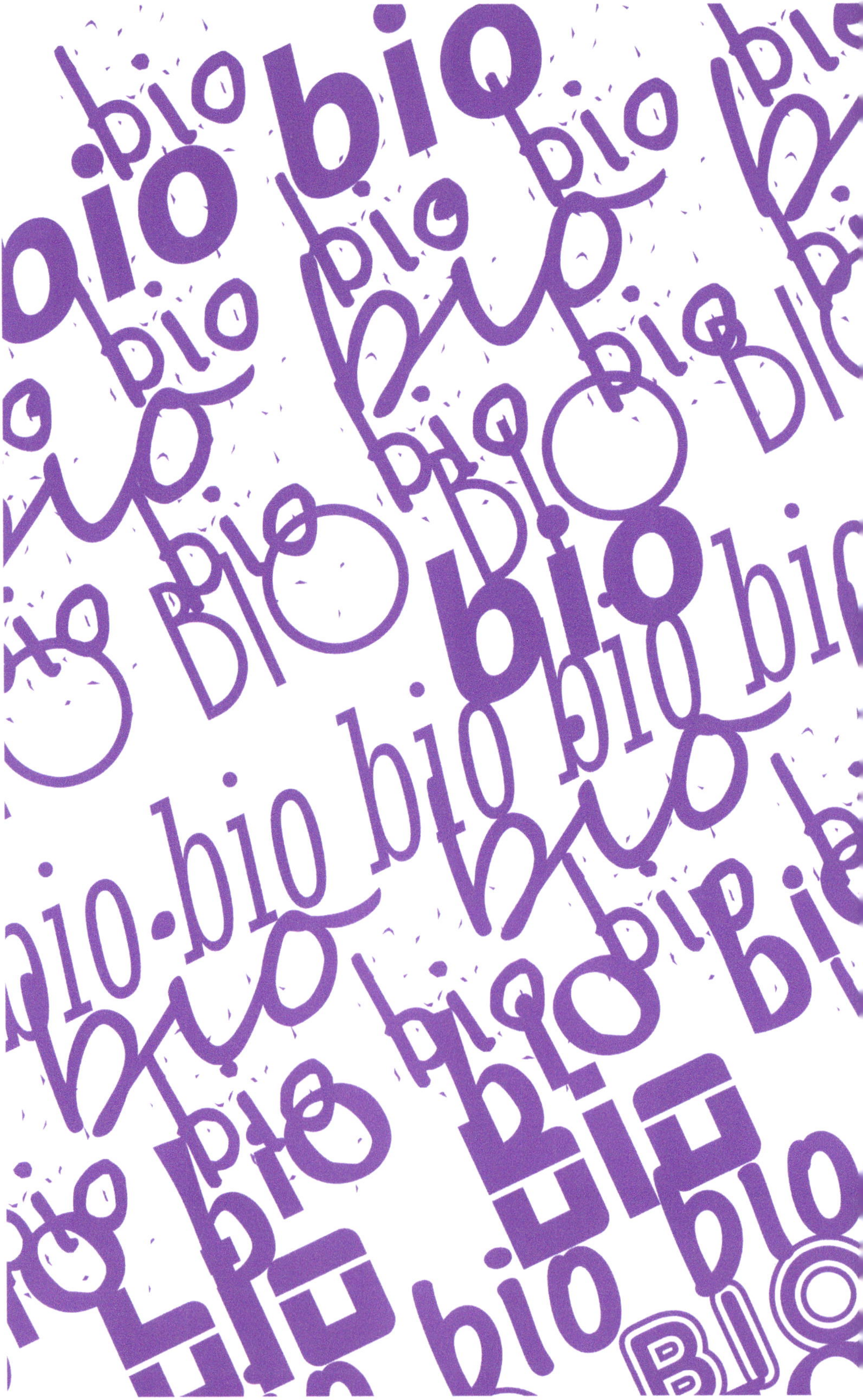
bio

Gwen Hullah co-author of this book

Past, present and future

=> farmers' daughter
=> instigator of Radio Witham (1976); station manager (1977 - 1987)
=> music manager for songwriter, Ida (2003 - 2010)
=> partner at book publisher, She And The Cat's Mother
=> novelist
=> screenwriter

For updates of Gwen's projects join us online at www.SilverSplitter.com

Hole Bottom Farms, Dacre, Nr Harrogate

Author Gwen Hullah's parents, Tommy and Ida Hullah owned and farmed Hole Bottom Farms for many years (and there giving birth to five daughters and one son). They were shorthorn dairy farmers - with sidelines of breeding large whites, sheep and free-range poultry.

Tommy & Ida Hullah's wedding day 1931

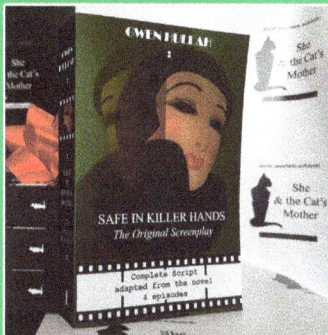

SAFE IN KILLER HANDS
The Original Screenplay
Complete script adapted from the novel 4 episodes

A CHANGE IS AS GOOD AS A REPLY
Mother and Daughter: Gwen and Ida establish book publisher, She And The Cat's Mother (2016)

Picture: Radio Witham receive cheque (1976)

As reported in the Grantham Journal: Helping "Radio Witham" a broadcasting service for Grantham Hospital patients, on its way. Officer Commanding R.A.F. Swinderby, Group Capt. D. Green, third from the left, hands a cheque for £164, raised by his men, to Mr R. Keightley, on behalf of the Friends of Grantham Hospital. Also in the picture, from the left, are Flt. Lieut. Ben Theed, Barry Mac, David Wood, Tessa Wood, Gwen Barker (nee Hullah) and Garry Wakefield

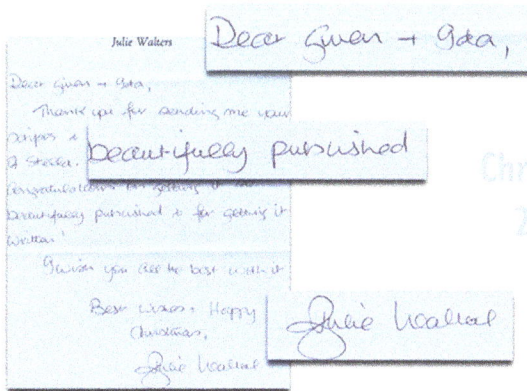

>> **ida:** live at The Boardwalk Sheffield 2008

A letter-of-praise from *Dame Julie Walters*
to book publishers, She And The Cat's Mother, for paperback,
SAFE IN KILLER HANDS: THE ORIGINAL SCREENPLAY

Complete letter below:

Follow the Romans to combat floods

In response to the Reeth, Grinton and Fremington floods, there is a workable solution to this devastating disturbance of nature as history shows - do as the Romans did

The Romans solution to prevent floods of destruction was to "fork" a natural stream or river by manually directing one of the two divides to flow away from communities, proprietors of properties and agricultural land

Furthermore, after each deluge, each waterway was cleared of the build up of slurry and debris. A safeguard against "flash flood" disasters

My grandfather and father, John and Thomas (Tommy) Hullah, farmed Hole Bottom Farms, Dacre Banks, near Harrogate, for many years. Two streams - one either side of adjoining farms - flowed peacefully on meeting but during continuous rainfall, clashed, bursting their banks before roaring away beneath the (listed) superior constructed three ached Roman bridge built beneath the cart road, (a hidden gem) to join the original stream which eventually flowed into the River Nidd

GH

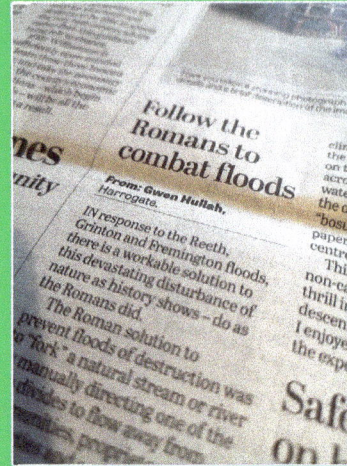

Photo by Ida Barker
of Gwen's published letter printed
in The Yorkshire Post

144

Ida Barker co-author and illustrator of this book

All in a day's work (at time of publishing, other roles include):

=> partner at book publisher, She And The Cat's Mother
=> barista and social media content creator for bookshop cafe Waterstones @HarrogateCafeW
=> home-shopper at ASDA supermarket
=> writing fiction using pseudonym Zizzi Bonah

Here's a sample of Ida's social media join us via facebook | twitter | instagram @IdaBarkerDotCom

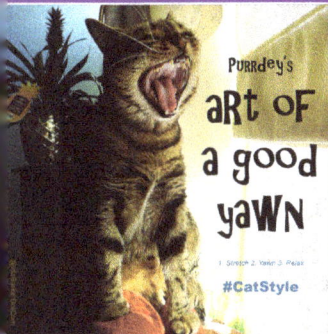

PURRdey's
aRT OF
a good
yaWN

1. Screen 2. Yawn 3. Paws

#CatStyle

GOLDEN TICKET

World
Book Day
5 March 2020
Waterstones
Harrogate

IAN: Whose songs should we add to our work playlist today?
IDA: Whitney Spears

EMMA: Who's your favourite James Bond?
IDA: Ooh, Craig David
EMMA: Hmm?

(i)

As mentioned on
Loose Women
ITV prog'

A pineapple plant will boost oxygen in a room, and is known to reduce snoring

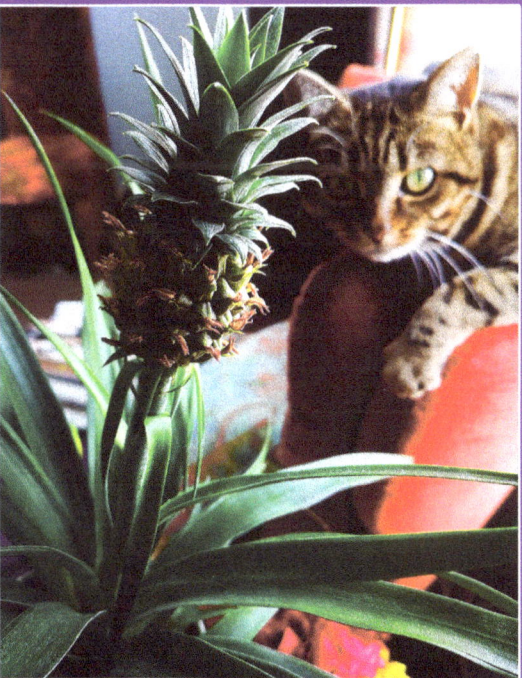

#MyCatSnores

Picture: Purrdey the cat, with plant bought using my staff discount card from Asda, Harrogate @idaBarkerDotCom

ASDA
indoor
PLANTS
ORNAMENTAL
PINEAPPLE PLANT
EASY TO CARE FOR
£10

(L-R) Ant, Lesley, Ida

The New Normal
#Asda #KeyWorkers #StaySafe #Covid19

On this page:
all photos and social media content created by Ida Barker
(except World Book Day photo of Ida with Keiran
Lancaster taken by bookseller, Rob Young
with Ida's camera-phone)

Sampling cake with Steff
@HarrogateCafeW

NEW festive drinks @HarrogateCafeW picture by Ida barker

Acorn Dairy We will not tell our Dairy Shorthorns what you do with their organic milk!
If you are short of milk now, give the office a call and we will top you up. Hope the clean up is swift. 😟

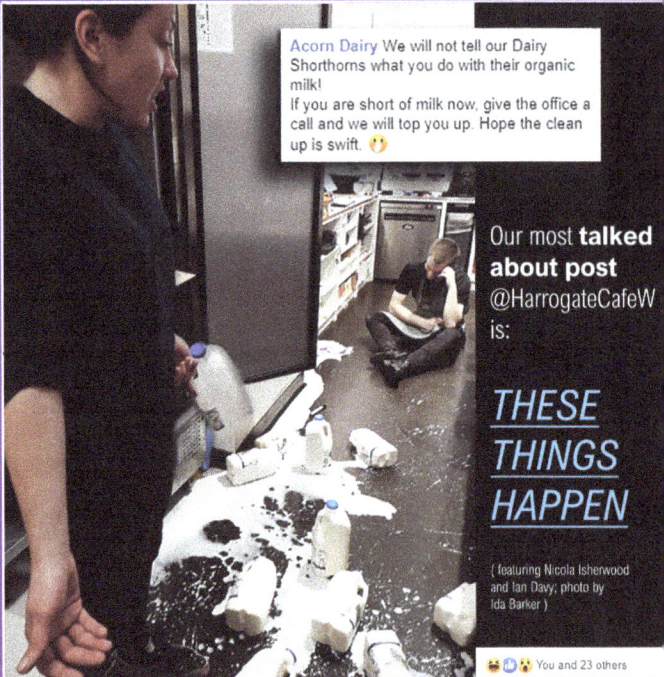

Our most **talked about post** @HarrogateCafeW is:

THESE THINGS HAPPEN

(featuring Nicola Isherwood and Ian Davy; photo by Ida Barker)

😆🙂😲 You and 23 others

Harry Potter Quiz

10.10.19

1st

Celebrating new illustrated edition
of
Harry Potter & the Goblet of Fire
we hosted a quiz for wizards
Quiz master: Keiran Lancaster

Winners:
1st - The Sorcerous Corrins
2nd - Team Careford
3rd - Team Dowie

This event was held at Harrogate bookshop Waterstones (1st floor within Cafe W)
Pictures by Ida Barker for @HarrogateCafeW

2nd

3rd

@HarrogateCafeW

FREE in-store drink when you BUY one of our books-of-the-month at Waterstones

THE DOLL FACTORY ELIZABETH MACNEAL

THE CHAIN

MARCH 2020
@HarrogateCafeW

Good News

Take-up Posts

Paula McCavanagh, Training & Merchandising Manager has requested to include some of Ida's @HarrogateCafeW media posts within "The Monthly Commercial update"

Steff Winter, Harrogate Cafe W Manager (left); Paula's email (middle); Ida Barker (right)

Give us a kiss !!

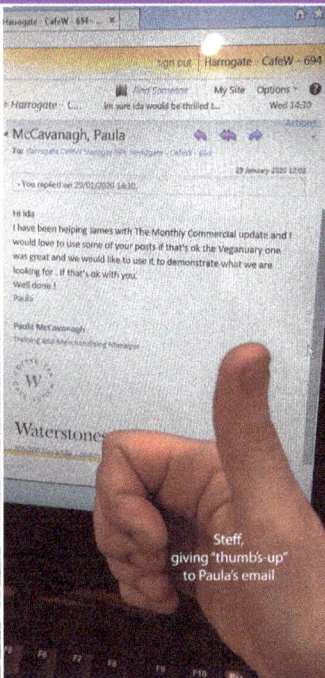

Steff, giving "thumb's-up" to Paula's email

"Good news" post on this page created and uploaded by Ida Barker to @HarrogateCafeW [Waterstones bookshop cafe]

August 8th 2020

LOVE DATE on the Pablo! course at Junkyard Golf Club with Jesse Ridgway

PURR-fect

mother's day

PURR-fect
Mother's day
published on Gwen's SilverSplitter.com

The business of being Mother

What a lovely surprise I had by way of a change from the usual shop bought Mother's day card, my splendid daughter, Ida, took this selfie with our cat, Purrdey and placed the image on a personalised card, courtesy of moonpig

Which reminded me of an amusing family tale:

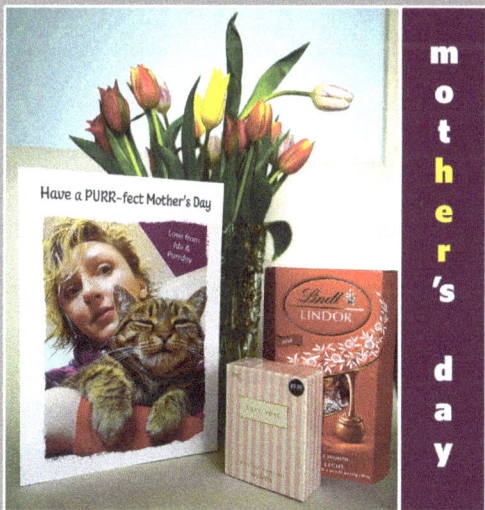

m o t h e r's d a y

Many years ago, my mother bought her mother a bunch of **asparagus** instead of the annual birthday bouquet of flowers. Grandma arranged them into a vase thinking they were bluebells

GH

Picture by @IdaBarkerDotCom
card purchased from moonpig.com; tulips ASDA; perfume Primark

" The presence of minds "

Books

by this publisher include ...

paperbacks | hardbacks | ebooks | audiobooks
by this publisher include:

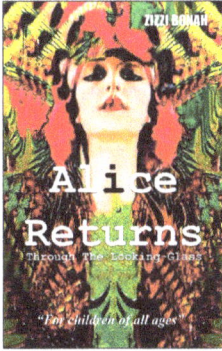

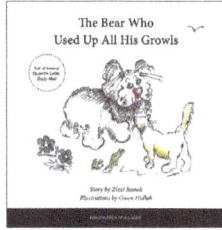

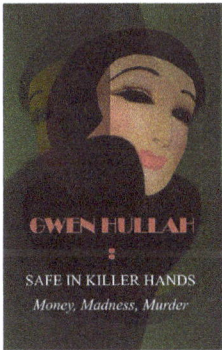

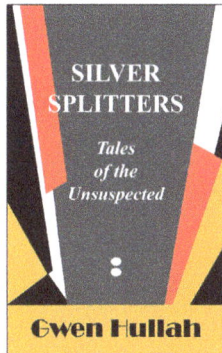

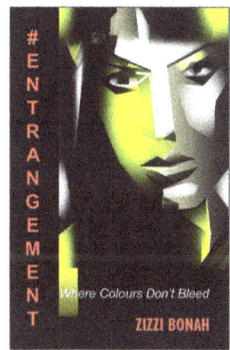

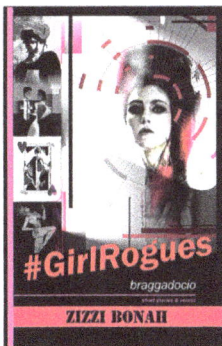

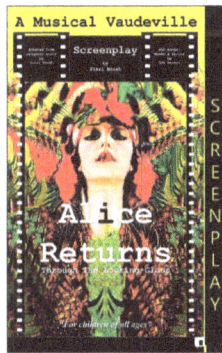

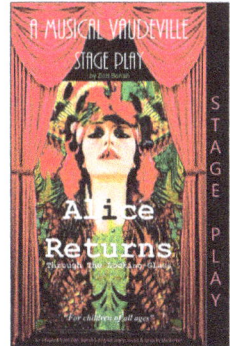

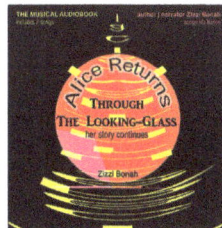

The Bear Who Used Up All His Growls

Story by Zizzi Bonah
Illustrations by Gwen Hullah

ZIZZI BONAH

Alice Returns
Through The Looking-Glass

"For children of all ages"

GWEN HULLAH
:
SAFE IN KILLER HANDS
The Original Screenplay

Complete Script
adapted from the novel
4 episodes

SILVER SPLITTERS
Tales of the Unsuspected
:
Gwen Hullah

GWEN HULLAH
:
SAFE IN KILLER HANDS
Money, Madness, Murder

#ENTRANGEMENT
Where Colours Don't Bleed
ZIZZI BONAH

A Musical Vaudeville
Screenplay
by Zizzi Bonah

Alice Returns
Through The Looking-Glass
"For children of all ages"
SCREENPLAY

A MUSICAL VAUDEVILLE
STAGE PLAY
by Zizzi Bonah

Alice Returns
Through The Looking-Glass
"For children of all ages"
STAGE PLAY

#GirlRogues
braggadocio
short stories & verses
ZIZZI BONAH

THE MUSICAL AUDIOBOOK
author | narrator Zizzi Bonah

Alice Returns
THROUGH THE LOOKING-GLASS
her story continues
Zizzi Bonah

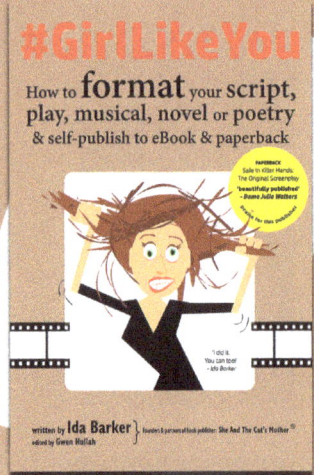

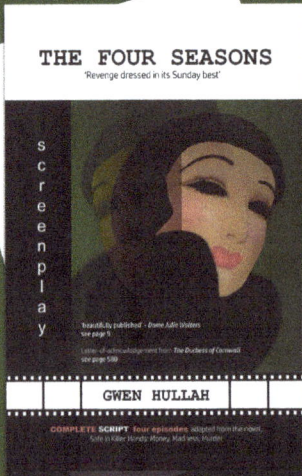

The following pages show photocopies

of the **first 12 SCENES** of Gwen Hullah's

screenplay, SAFE IN KILLER HANDS

The complete script, 4 episodes, is available at amazon
in ebook and paperback; adapted from Gwen's debut novel,
Safe In Killer Hands: Money, Madness, Murder

Also published as a special paperback edition,
under the title, THE FOUR SEASONS

EPISODE 1

WINTER

SCENE 1

EXT. YORKSHIRE - WINTER RURAL LANDSCAPE - 3:15 PM

The year is 1947. We see vast acreage of desolate winter-white moorland, then sight lower-land where blackfaced sheep shelter behind stone walls, their fleeces congealed with icy-snow - stillness broken occasionally by their haunting bleating.

SCENE 2

EXT. STOCKDALE FARMS - 3:16 PM

Two adjoining stone farmhouses with attached outer buildings silhouetted against snow laden sky. Dim lights seen from three windows. We are drawn down to a snow-banked beck aligned with gaunt trees; to stepping stones; flagged water-splash; towards icicle waterfall. We view dark depth to copious flow beyond.

SCENE 3

INT. STOCKDALE FARMS - STELLA'S LIVING ROOM - 3:17 PM

Furnished with over-large furniture. A full sized black leaded fireplace, surrounded by horse brasses and rosettes.

We see STELLA ASQUITH, aged 46, handsome, proud woman with naturally wavy ginger-red hair which frames vivacious features. She is sat rigid at bureau, pen in hand. Suddenly rises. Goes over to window and stares outwards.

SCENE 4
EXT. STOCKDALE FARMS - MOORLAND - DAY (FLASHBACK)

We see SAM ASQUITH, aged 72, tall formidable man, alienated, staggering blindly through violent snow blizzard wholly exhausted - falling - rising to finally fall into contracted position, frozen through death's open door.

SCENE 5
EXT. STOCKDALE FARMS - MOORLAND - DAY (FLASHBACK)

Three days after fatal blizzard.

We see and hear JAKE SWALES, aged 65, farm-man, stoic, vigorous with psycho-tendency - shabbily dressed, overcoat has no belt, hanging loose revealing worn trousers strung chest high by faded braces exposing long-legged boots, and ABE ASQUITH, aged 64, less-fortunate-begrudging cousin of SAM, a large man, deadpan expression, rarely smiles.

Shovels in hands, hacking, digging, scraping - SAM'S body being prised from ice-bound grave.

SCENE 6
INT. STOCKDALE FARMS - STELLA'S LIVING ROOM - 3:18 PM

STELLA turns away from window. Her face creased in sorrow. Returns to desk and dates letter page, 24TH JANUARY 1947.

SCENE 7
EXT. COUNTRY ROADS - TWO WEEKS LATER - 2 PM

We see snowplough reopening snow-bound country roads. Blizzards filling in the cuttings almost as fast as man and machine can dig. They decide to call it a day.

EXT. STOCKDALE FARMS - MAIN GATE ENTRANCE - 3 PM

GRACE ASQUITH, aged 26, a smallish woman, neither frail nor chunky, phenomenally strong willed, known for speaking her own mind, yet has sensitivity she rarely puts into words.

We see GRACE zigzagging a route in deep uncut slip-road. She heads for main gate entrance. Rubs coat sleeve over gate sign: STOCKDALE FARMS, hitches rucksack to other shoulder, turns up overcoat collar, shivers, climbs up and over gate wedged by snowdrift and heads home along the mile-long cart-road.

SCENE 9

INT. STOCKDALE FARMS - STELLA'S KITCHEN - 4 PM

Large kitchen. Flag-stoned floor. No electricity or gas supplies and no hot water flows.

STELLA is ladling hot water from back boiler into a bucket. We hear the lifting of the iron door sneck, then the dull drop, we see the draft of snowflakes as GRACE pushes door open to vacillate inside. She bangs it shut, leaving herself on the inside.

> STELLA
> *(pleasantly)*
> I knew you'd come ... given time ...
> but not to put too fine a point on it
> our Grace, you'd rather be late than
> wrong.

STELLA drops the boiler lid down and places wet jug on the hot surface where it sizzles away - unnoticed to them.

GRACE removes rucksack, then headscarf. She runs her fingers through her damp hair.

                    GRACE
          It's hard to be punctual in the snow,
          Mother.

There's no overbearing welcome between them, only a toughness and philosophical attitude. Love is known, no need to be said.

STELLA carries bucket of hot water to the sink and pours half into sink bowl.

                    STELLA
          I've missed you over the last two
          years, more than I can ever say ...
                    *(she dashes soap flakes into
                    bowl and stirs vigorously)*
          Easy enough when I carry a private
          conversation in my head ...
                    (she smiles)
          At least I can say, thank God you've
          arrived home safely which is more than
          I can say about your father ...
                    (smile wavers)
          We could tell by his footprints in the
          snow that he'd been crossing and re-
          crossing the frozen-over beck trying
          to locate the fort shelter ...
                    (her voice quails)
          Cousin Abe said Sam had most likely
          become disoriented by the snow
          blizzard ...

                    GRACE
          (takes overcoat off and drapes
          it over wooden clothes horse)
Uncle Abe and Aunt Winny, as Grandma
Blanche said last week ...
          (scornfully)
have the belief that Father, the elder
Cousin, would bequest them an
adjoining farm, knowing you and Father
have no son to pass it onto just to
keep the Asquith name alive in the
farming community!

                    STELLA
          (washing crockery)
I believe you're right Grace, and I
may be wrong, but I'm certain that Abe
took perverse pleasure in breaking
your father's limbs so he and Jake
could lay him flat on the field gate,
and the rope ...
          (her voice breaks)
the cart rope was not equal to the
purpose of securing Sam to the gate
spars ...
          (voice rises)
then to crown it all, he had the
asperity to say ...
          (she swallows her pain)
"By Gawd! He looks more human dead
than ever he did alive!"

                    GRACE
And Jake ...?
          (sits down at table)
Did he rise to the insinuation?

STELLA

Too shocked. Never known him so quiet.
Hardly spoke a word. His answer was to
barge over to Bonny then back her
within inches of the gate ...

> (pause)

Abe took the chain traces from the
horse's harness and hitched them onto
the gate hinges ...

> (begins to wipe plates dry)

I led Bonny while the men hauled on
side-ropes to prevent the gate
striking the back of Bonny's limbs by
sliding forward on the icy ground ...

We hear crockery clatter as STELLA stacks them onto cupboard
shelves ...

STELLA

As for Jake, well, he was quite
unchaste, more so than when his wife
died of shingles.

> (pause)

He did say after working and living
alongside the Asquiths for near on
fifty years, he'd never once thought
it would come to this.

GRACE

> (suddenly vacates chair, words
> bitter to taste)

Money talks! Money can whitewash!
That's what Father use to say, but
death was one deal he couldn't buy his
way out of, as Grandma Blanche said,
"Hell won't want him because he'd take

control"!

GRACE abruptly leaves the room.

STELLA stretches her arms out to her and gathers emptiness.
We see grief expressed unguarded.

SCENE 10
EXT. STOCKDALE FARMS – TOP COW-HOUSE – 6 PM

Tilly lamps glowing from inside a cow-house window. We
glimpse JAKE shabbily dressed wearing hobnailed boots walking
towards the building. He is carrying a milk bucket on crook
of his arm and a storm lamp in one hand and a three legged
stool in the other hand. He enters the building.

SCENE 11
INT. STOCKDALE FARMS – TOP COW-HOUSE – 6:01 PM

We see SOPHIE ASQUITH, aged 22, gentle by nature, a wholesome
girl but splendidly indiscreet, and STELLA already hand-
milking TWO OF TWELVE DAIRY COWS chained by the neck within
individual wooden stalls.

JAKE strides across the manure channel behind cattle, plonks
his stool down by RHODA'S hindquarters, sits down, rams
bucket between his legs to rest rim on his heels. Shoves his
flat capped head onto RHODA'S flank while endeavouring to
pull and squeeze on two opposite teats.

We hear occasional lowly "mooing" and the steady rhythm of
the ejecting milk as it penetrates into the depths of the
already drawn down milk within their three buckets.

11

INT. STOCKDALE FARMS - STELLA'S LIVING ROOM - 7:30 PM

STELLA is placing logs on fire as GRACE enters, washed and re-dressed in khaki dungarees and multifarious fair-isle jumper.

>   STELLA
>   *(turns round and half-smiles*
>   *sadly)*
> Your name never passed your father's
> lips again, and dear Sophie, every now
> and then, she'd wear that jumper
> Grandma Blanche knitted for you years
> ago, as an indication of keeping you
> close to her. She really has missed
> her older sister more than words could
> ever say ...

>   GRACE
> Yes, my leaving was with the distinct
> feeling of separateness ...
>   *(pause)*
> Do you think Father suffered a great
> deal between the difference of life
> and death?

She crosses the room to turn the wireless knob to the HOME SERVICE.

>   GRACE
> And do we know when we do something
> for the last time?

STELLA turns back to fire and rakes poker through bottom grate.

                    STELLA
        Hard to say, lass. He was very much
        dead when we found him ... and when I
        took my last look at your father
        before Cousin Abe screwed down the lid
        of his coffin, I saw that his face was
        covered by his overcoat ... and when I
        lifted it from his face, his eyes were
        open. He was looking straight back at
        me ...
                    (her voice catches her throat)
        And I wanted to keep him here where he
        belonged, instead I said to Abe that
        Sam should be wearing it, because he
        would feel the cold. Abe pulled me
        aside and said ...
                    (her voice falters)
        "He doesn't belong to you anymore".

STELLA brushes away excess ash from hot fire-bars, then turns
to look at GRACE.

                    STELLA
        But I will say this, you're a sure
        reminder to me ...
                    (pause)
        A smaller image of course - that Sam
        Asquith is not completely dead.

We hear muted voices coming from wireless.

They go unheard to STELLA and GRACE.

                    GRACE
        The more I think about it, the more I
        believe death is the absent one who

                            13

sees to it that family business will
remain unfinished.

                STELLA
            (drops another log on the fire)
    And goodbyes remain unspoken forever
    and a day. Your father was no good at
    writing letters because he was already
    very skilful at hiding his feelings
    and dealings ...
            (her eyes reflect anger and
            heartache)
    If only Sam had shown more of his
    heart ...

                GRACE
            (bitterly)
    Instead of showing a lack of interest
    that was calculated to dishearten all
    but the fanatical.

GRACE folds her arms tightly across her breasts and sits down
on sofa. Her eyes meet her mother's in a polished stare,
faces claiming a portion of quiet desperation that is not
altogether quiet, displayed in a succession of disturbances
of faint moans, tormented grunts and unguarded coughing.

From across the room, like an uninvited guest, the HOME
SERVICE NEWS ANNOUNCER gives out a warning ...

                HOME SERVICE (WIRELESS)
    Look out for helicopters dropping food
    and animal provisions over the cut-off
    areas ...
            (voice more authoritative)
    German Prisoners of War have arrived

> on camp sites in the North of England
> and these men are being placed at the
> disposal of the Highway Surveyors to
> aid snow clearances ...

GRACE springs swiftly from the sofa. Switches off wireless.
One suffering expression superimposed on another. Her mouth
hardily moves at all.

> GRACE
> I remember the day I left home,
> remember how slowly I reacted when
> Father said Hertz had hung himself
> from a beam in the bottom barn, and I
> don't think that I was convinced at
> the time – but I was ready to believe
> anything when the alternative was so
> unbelievable ...
>> *(turns distressed face to the*
>> *wall)*
> And ... and ... feeling within myself
> a sense of loss so ... so deep that it
> shook my soul.

STELLA comes to stand close to GRACE'S rigid back and slowly
wraps her arms around her.

FLASH – We see a young POW hanging from a beam in the barn.
Castrated. Accentuated by the beams of sunlight filtering
from the narrow slat glassless windows to depict SAM and
JAKE, slowly they turn to stare coldly at STELLA standing
transfixed within the doorway ...

FADE TO DARKNESS.

stacks 5 Page.
(11 Pages.) = Page 15 ✓

15 ✓

Gwen Hullah's,
SAFE IN KILLER HANDS
complete script (4 episodes)
available NOW at amazon
in ebook and paperback

Also published as a special paperback edition,
under the title, THE FOUR SEASONS

READ a section from #Entrangement by Zizzi Bonah:

Sensing I am alone now, I open my eyes and confirm there is nothing between myself and the flickering source of candle light, only the book - I reach down and take its edge.

Moments ago, a prison guard hurled the book into my cell - tauting words followed - according to common wisdom it's unlucky for a prisoner to read their own book of life. The truth is - I am my own woman, and anyone who claims I am not, professes to know a different me!

I lower the book, letting the candlelight shine onto it. The title reads: Prisoner Of The Past: Salt Delray. I open it, but am bedazzled by dancing light and shadows. Only a stir of knowing reaches up from the pages; and I'm transfixed, seemingly recognising the outline of words. The book becomes heavier in my hands as new pages and chapters are added to the volume - it appears to be writing itself.

I take the candle and move it close to the book. The hot wax drips onto the pages. the liquid runs, spelling out words as it presses and cools to congeal. It has written: If you sit very still, you can hear the sun move. The meaning doesn't resonate to me. Then I gasp, sighting a kiss from the flame to the book's corner. Instantly my fingers fly to knockback the fire, but the book has already changed into charred paper, unravelling wisps drift upwards and out through my prison cell window, towards the setting sola sun.

Turning my face to the wall, despair escapes me which isn't silent. I only hope my instincts aren't as close as far away. For I have read of a time and a place yet to be lived - the future. If I'm right, and this isn't a cruel deception, then my life will continue.

But if I'm wrong?

The cell door bangs open. I wheel round.

A prison guard rasps, "It's time!"

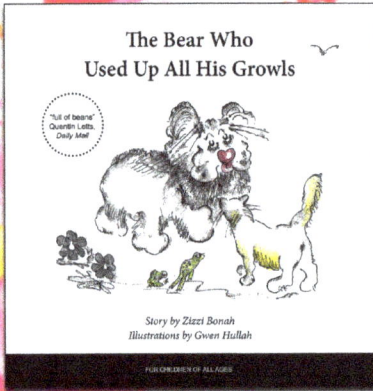

Here's the opening lines from the book,
The Bear Who Used Up All His Growls by Zizzi Bonah:

In a retreat; a place shaded from the sun and next to a flowing stream warmed by the breezes —— lived a Bear. Every morning, as a ritual, Bear would guard away unwelcome visitors with a very loud growl; so loud a growl that the tamarind trees and dandelion-clock clouds would awaken with such a start, they would swerve apart, allowing Bear a clear view of the mountains over Yonder Valley.

All the creatures who lived in and around Yonder Valley would say to one another, "To concentrate too much attention upon one's territory may cause one to tumble into it. Where are the Bear's manners? Does he not realise kindness is inclusive, whereas selfishness is exclusive?"

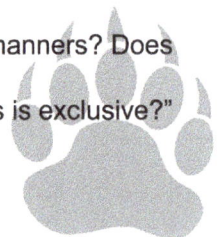

Meet lugubrious Bear
and his unlikely companions
(who could not be more tribally different)

LUGUBRIOUS BEAR - a fearless bear who guards his territory, Yonder Valley with ferocity - that is until the letter O drops clean out of his resounding growl

PURDY - a sophisticated cat who knows the value of common playfulness, supported by reason and probabilities

EEBYGUMOLOGISTS - notoriously outspoken creatures, skilled with glorious wit and sparkling insight

JUSTICE NINCOMPOOP - precocious girlish-girl assassin, with inside knowledge of Bear's peccadilloes!

DOTTY HIPPO - a pillar of society, but splendidly indiscreet

Perhaps territorial Bear, who has never been interested in befriending nomad creatures, will learn about comradeship and tidy manners, while travelling to the County of Vowels; Justice Nincompoop's homestead - but will the justice refuse or award Machiavellian Bear a licence of O's?

SILVER SPLITTERS

*Tales
of the
Unsuspected*

:

Gwen Hullah

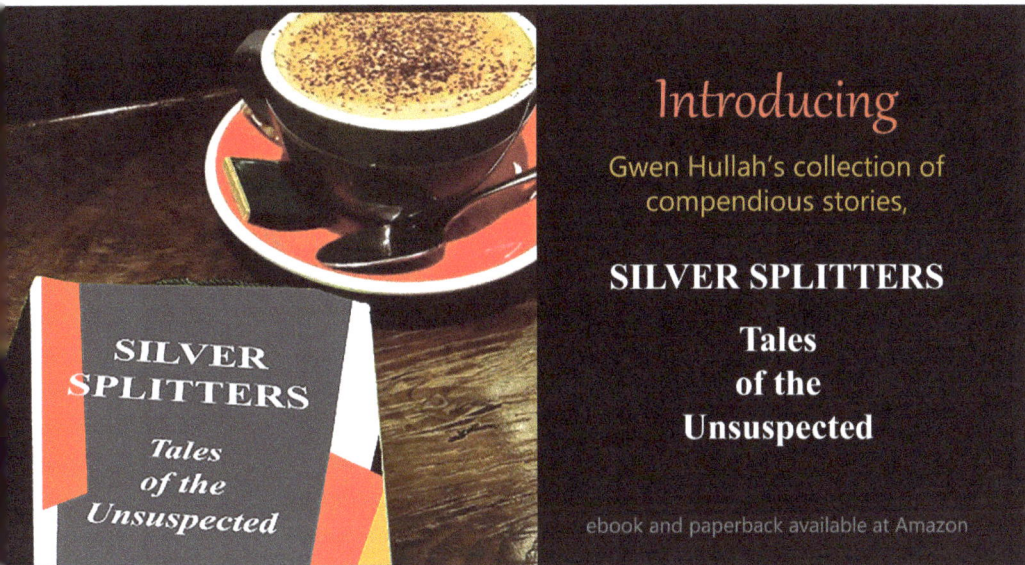

Meet the shameless women of a certain age who kick over the traces in the most unsuspected way

She Kissed It Worse, a very plain widow with very deliberate ways; who knows the value of medicinal herbs and deadly plants ...

Daggers Drawn, a Women's Institute secretary who takes perverse pleasure in usurping an old rival - the reinstated chairwomen, and finds herself much read about in a most unsuspected way ...

Keen To Shoehorn, where a wife's ultimatum leads to a husband's ultimate trap ...

Spaghetti Hat, a sophisticated lady who knows the worth of simplicity, wherein, connections between her alibi must not be examined ...

=> these stories and more within, SLIVER SPLITTERS: Tales of the Unsuspected by Gwen Hullah

ZIZZI BONAH

Alice Returns
Through The Looking-Glass

"For children of all ages"

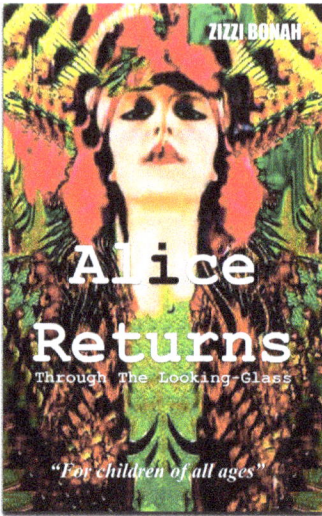

**EBOOK AND PAPERBACK
AVAILABLE AT AMAZON**

A story wherein every goodbye isn't gone, and every eye shut isn't sleep. Alice must find the answer to the Looking-Glass question - much to the rage of infamous book reviewer, Paige Turner who threatens to jeopardise **Alice's writing career in Authorland!**

Hoodlemania descends and together Alice and her predatory blonde alter-ego, **Miss Penopause** walk the **Critical Path** to set fore-running hazards and high-jinks in motion, in a bid to make **Paige Turner eat her words** and silence the damning book review before publication - but at what cost?

For as Alice learns; it is far easier to get forgiveness than it is to get Paige Turner!

All characters in this story are the creation of Zizzi Bonah (with exception to Alice, who was created by Lewis Carroll)

All songs featured in this story are written (both words and music) by Ida Barker

I look forward to discovering more about Alice's adventures

- HRH the Duchess of Cornwall

HERE'S AN EXTRACT FROM CHAPTER 8, WRITTEN BY ZIZZI BONAH

ALICE RETURNS
THROUGH THE LOOKING–GLASS

"Oh, yes," said Alice. "I think I have quite got into the habit of asking the ask instead of doing the do." Then reaching down to the dandelion clock, she said quite plainly, in case the dandelion clock was in any doubt to her meaning. "I will have to forcefully exhale on you, my dear. And the number of exhales it takes for all your hair to fly off your head and away on the breeze, will tell us the number of the time."

"For all the petals in Rosemead," protested the dandelion clock. "I have never known such obtrusive behaviour in all my life! If you knew about character-isation, you would know it is acted out through one's behaviour and desires, from the first to the last, in order to be believable."

"Here, here," said another dandelion clock just off by the thicket. "And overmore, if you intend to take the time where exactly do you plan on keeping it?"

"Now look here," said Alice to the second dandelion clock. "I have no argument with you."

"I should think not!" protested the second. "It is most rude to go around picking arguments with plant life when you haven't substantiated the present picking. And I maybe short-sighted, but even I can see you have no vase to place your pickings in."

This original story by Zizzi, now adapted to a musical vaudeville stage play and also screenplay in ebook and paperback, praise for the stage play book "full of beans" - Quentin Letts, Art Critic

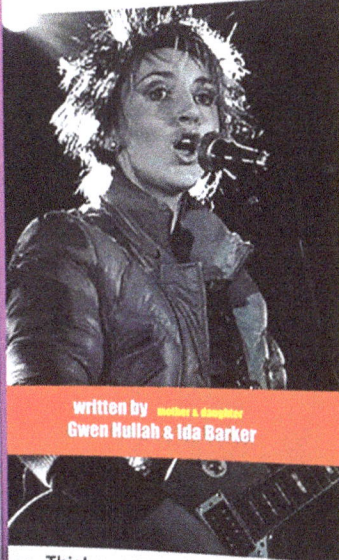

Your notes

from your head to your hands:
write your ideas down

@RaffleProperty

@RaffleProperty

@RaffleProperty

JOIN the conversation

@RaffleProperty

@RaffleProperty

@RaffleProperty

@RaffleProperty

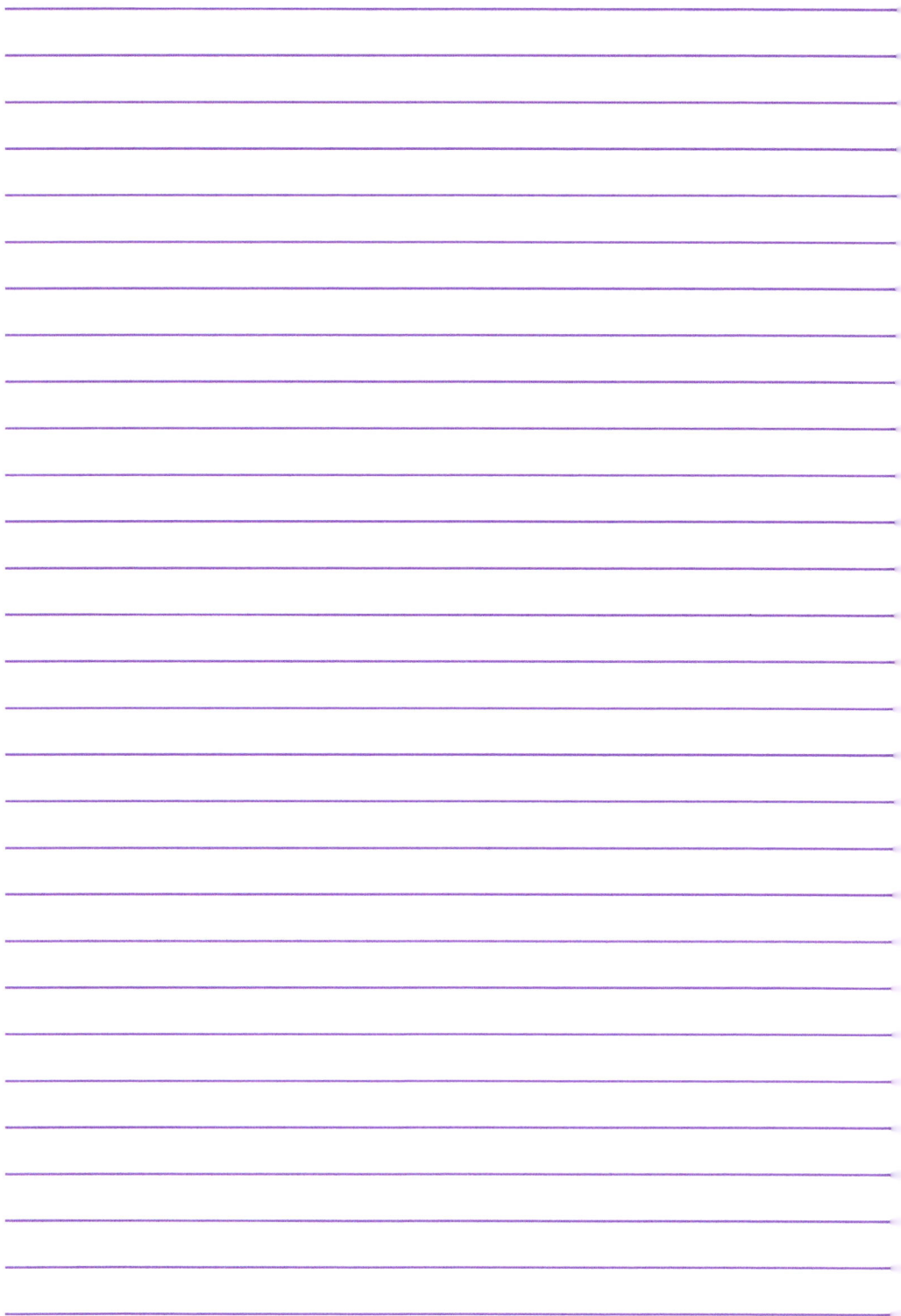

JOIN
the conversation

£

@RaffleProperty

@RaffleProperty

@RaffleProperty

@RaffleProperty

@RaffleProperty

Raffle Property

You're invited

Share your raffle property and house competition stories

We'd love to hear which property events you have entered or organised

How have you found the process so far?

Join the conversation
facebook | twitter | instagram
@RaffleProperty

Photo: Ida Barker (R); Gwen Hullah (L); www.RaffleProperty.net

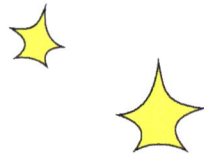

Thank you
for reading our alternative book